Charles John Perry

Spiritual perspective and other sermons

Charles John Perry

Spiritual perspective and other sermons

ISBN/EAN: 9783337085841

Printed in Europe, USA, Canada, Australia, Japan

Cover: Foto ©Andreas Hilbeck / pixelio.de

More available books at **www.hansebooks.com**

SPIRITUAL PERSPECTIVE

AND OTHER SERMONS

BY THE LATE

CHARLES JOHN PERRY, B.A.,

MINISTER OF
HOPE STREET CHURCH, LIVERPOOL.

EDITED BY

R. A. ARMSTRONG, B.A.

LIVERPOOL:
HENRY YOUNG, 12, SOUTH CASTLE STREET.

1885.

BEDFORD:

PRINTED AT THE MERCURY PRESS.

PREFATORY NOTE.

The Discourses of Mr. Perry published, with a Memoir, early in the present year, were to a large extent "occasional" sermons, delivered in connection with some special event or day or institution. It is thought, however, that Mr. Perry's pulpit deliverances were, by reason of their simplicity and directness and their freedom from marked personal idiosyncrasies, of a kind unusually well adapted for use by lay preachers, or parents conducting services at home; such workers often being reluctant to rely on their own compositions, yet finding much difficulty in meeting with printed sermons entirely suitable to their purpose. In the selection of the present Sermons the want thus indicated has throughout been kept in view. While, therefore, all these Sermons are such as are well remembered for their beauty and force by those who heard them, they are all such as may be redelivered on any Sunday in the year.

The manuscripts from which they are printed bear occasional acknowledgments of indebtedness to Robertson, of Brighton, Robert Collyer, Brooke Herford, and other preachers of a liberal faith. It has not been thought necessary to investigate the exact measure of the influences thus referred to.

Charles John Perry was born at Bulwell, near Nottingham, in June, 1852, became Minister of the Hope Street Church, Liverpool, in September, 1878, and passed away on October the 9th, 1883.

Liverpool, December, 1884.

CONTENTS.

                                                                PAGE

I.—SPIRITUAL PERSPECTIVE 7

        Ye pay tithe of mint and anise and cummin, and have omitted the weightier matters of the law, judgment, mercy and faith.—MATT. xxiii., 23.

II.—THE STRAIT GATE 14

        Enter ye in by the narrow gate; for wide is the gate and broad is the way that leadeth to destruction, and many be they that enter in thereby. For narrow is the gate and straitened the way that leadeth unto life, and few be they that find it.—MATT. vii., 13-14.

III.—SELF-SACRIFICE 21

        For whosoever will save his life shall lose it; and whosoever will lose his life for my sake shall find it.—MATT. xvi., 25.

IV.—MODERN "SEEKING AFTER A SIGN" 28

        And when the people were gathered thick together, he began to say: This is an evil generation: they seek a sign; and there shall no sign be given it, but the sign of Jonas the prophet.—LUKE xi., 29.

V.—I WILL FOLLOW THEE, BUT— 36

        And another also said, Lord, I will follow thee; but let me first go bid them farewell, which are at home at my house. And Jesus said unto him, No man, having put his hand to the plough and looking back, is fit for the kingdom of God.—LUKE ix., 61, 62.

VI.—THE RUSH OF LIFE 44

        And he said unto them, Come ye yourselves apart into a desert place, and rest a while: for there were many coming and going, and they had no leisure so much as to eat.—MARK vi., 31.

VII.—FRANCIS OF ASSISI 51

        Seek ye first the kingdom of God, and his righteousness; and all these things shall be added unto you.—MATT. vi., 33.

	PAGE
VIII.—Sunshine	59

    Truly the light is sweet, and a pleasant thing it is for the eyes to behold the sun.—Eccles. xi., 7.

IX.—Is Life worth Living?	66

    Having promise of the life that now is, and of that which is to come.—I. Timothy iv., 8.

X.—Indifference	74

    I know thy works, that thou hast a name that thou livest, and art dead.—Rev. iii., 1.

XI.—Comfort in Religion	81

    The God of all comfort.—II. Corinthians i., 3.

XII.—With all your Heart	89

    Ye shall seek me, and find me, when ye shall search for me with all your heart.—Jeremiah xxix., 13.

XIII.—Faith Overcoming the World	97

    For whatsoever is born of God overcometh the world: and this is the victory that overcometh the world, even our faith.—I. John v., 3.

I.

Spiritual Perspective.

Ye pay tithe of mint and anise and cummin, and have omitted the weightier matters of the law, judgment, mercy and faith.—MATT. xxiii., 23.

THIS saying was addressed to Scribes and Pharisees. As a class, they were given to make religion too much a matter of outward forms and ceremonies—too little a matter of the heart. There were no doubt Pharisees and Pharisees; and an idea of Pharisaism derived from the New Testament alone would probably be exceedingly unjust. But still, making every allowance and giving them credit for a large measure of real earnestness and real goodness, there can be no doubt that the average Pharisee was far too much engrossed with ceremonial considerations, with conduct rather than with character, with ritual rather than with moral uprightness: and Jesus, with his perception that it is character which gives to conduct its abiding grace and glory, laid his finger at once upon this want of proportion in the prevailing views of duty and religion, and tried to make people discern more clearly what things were of real importance and what were comparatively insignificant.

The Pharisees, as a class, seemed to have no idea of moral perspective. This was a serious fault—as you will see, if you will compare morals for a moment with art. The artistic productions of nations in their infancy are often almost unintelligible, or exceedingly ludicrous, on account of the entire absence of a knowledge of perspective. If you have ever noticed copies of Chinese or old Egyptian drawings you will have seen how utterly at a loss the artists were to represent comparative distances, and how the drawings fail to be pictures in consequence. Or look at an ordinary willow-pattern plate. Probably you will agree that, with all its economic merits, it has grave defects as a work of art. There is no true perspective. The house in the distance is as large as that in the foreground, and the water fowl several miles off are as big as the children close by. The Chinese have not yet discovered the laws by which the size and forms of objects must be modified in order to throw them into their right places in a picture and to give the effect of distance.

Now, in mental and spiritual things, there are laws analogous to this law of perspective. The wise man is he whose thoughts obey these laws, whose mind groups its materials in this orderly fashion, and who therefore can see clearly and distinctly what is practically important and what is not. Success in business, I fancy, depends very much upon knowing what to do first, and what to postpone or leave undone. A great general is he who sees clearly the main points and lines of a campaign, and will not be confused or diverted by the multitude of side issues and details. Listen to the pleading of an eminent barrister in a court of law. There is a great mass of confused and conflicting testimony; and inexperienced listeners can form no clear opinion as to the facts at issue. He takes it all in hand, sets the important facts in a clear light in the foreground; lets the less important matters fall back into the middle distance; and throws the unessential evidence into the dim background. And so, by simply arranging his material in accordance with a kind of perspective law, he enables his listeners to see the real drift of the evidence, and makes out a clear and convincing case.

The opposite effect is seen in books and sermons and speeches and conversation, which, though their matter may be excellent, have no order and proportion about them, treat trivial gossip as though it were equally important with the affairs of the nation, and lack beginning, middle or end. An unordered, ill-balanced book or speech is always wearisome and ineffective, no matter how admirable its single sentences, or how true its individual thoughts.

But there is not only this intellectual perspective, there is a moral or spiritual perspective also, which determines the relative values of duties and virtues, and which is essential to a well-ordered character and life. It was this which the Pharisees lacked. Their picture was all foreground. They thought the tithing of mint and anise and cummin more important than justice, mercy and faith. They brought the little ceremonies which ought to have been kept in the background to the front, and painted them in so large and in such strong colours that they completely hid the great principles and feelings which ought to have been the main features of the scene; and thus the higher duties of life were omitted and forgotten, and attention was given wholly to unimportant trifles. It is a weakness of conscience not confined to Pharisees, not unknown amongst Englishmen even to-day. Do we never think overmuch of times and seasons? How is it, then, that we go on keeping the Sabbath-day holy by shutting up our libraries and picture-galleries and museums, and are content meanwhile to leave great masses of the people drinking in the gin shops and lounging at the corners of the streets? If we understood that it is very unimportant in the sight of God how the Sunday be outwardly observed, but very important that on that and all other days men should be upright and sober and devout, surely we should not hesitate to break a mere conventionality in order to bring about a greater uprightness and sobriety amongst large masses of men.

Do Englishmen never think overmuch about the importance of mere matters of ritual? What is the meaning then of the intense excitement produced by the innovations or vagaries of a few Ritualistic clergymen? I do not defend their doings; but I venture to say that we should have no riots in churches, and no agitation meetings, and no cry of "the Church in danger" if, instead of introducing a procession or adopting the eastward position, these clergymen had lived idle, selfish, overbearing lives, or had suffered their congregations to die of spiritual neglect. It is not the weightier matters of the law that are uppermost in the thoughts of the excited Orangemen who constitute themselves defenders of the faith.

Again, think how people exaggerate the importance of matters of doctrine as compared with character. They think it a most dangerous thing to doubt the dogma of the Trinity or to question the theory of vicarious atonement; but, comparatively speaking, a small matter to be grasping and mean and underhand in business. It is no sin, they think, to hurl bitter and uncharitable denunciations against those who are not of their own Church or party; but a dreadful sin to go to a church which does not hold the opinions which they happen to hold themselves.

Again, in matters of religious observance how commonly some very little things are still represented as though they were very large. Take the rite of Baptism. Many Church of England clergymen will hardly give Christian burial to an unchristened child; and there are still hundreds of people who half, if not altogether, believe that baptism may make all the difference between salvation and damnation. The superstitious mother thinks it best to be on the safer side and has her sickly child baptized in haste, lest the omission should decide its fate in the life to come.

These are but illustrations of the way in which people forget all that Christ has said about obedience, self-sacrifice, humility, love, being the essence of religion. To Jesus, life—a holy, loving, self-denying life—was the one thing needful. By hundreds and hundreds of those who to-day call themselves his disciples, some opinion, some ceremony, some profession, belonging to some church, adhering to some religious usage, is given a more important place. What shall we say of such people? How shall we explain such wide deviation from the teaching of Christ? Shall we say that they are hypocrites, that they are consciously false to their Master's Gospel, that their narrowness and small-mindedness is a sin? I think not. I do not think that would be either charitable or true. I believe the simple explanation is that their thought is confused, that they really do not discern the relative importance of spiritual things, that in a word, they have no sense of spiritual perspective: so that if you could put their opinions on religion and morals into a picture, it would resemble, in its want of proportion, the drawing on a willow-pattern plate.

Well, but if this be no culpable sin, it is a very disastrous failing. Immense harm is done in the world by confusing great and small, important and trivial, in the matter of common duties and faults. The social standard of life is twisted and distorted and quite different from the real divine standard, and society palliates sins which God severely punishes, and severely punishes actions which are no sins at all in the clear eye of an Eternal Justice. This confusion begins very often with the teachings of childhood. Parents and those who have the charge of children are very apt to visit trivial acts of mere carelessness or thoughtlessness with the same amount of moral indignation as they would conduct that is actually wrong. If we are to judge by the amount of indignation displayed or punishment administered, children are taught that it is just as wrong to break a cup or a plate as it is to tell a lie, that to tear their clothes is quite as bad a piece of conduct as being cruel or selfish; and the consequence is that either they grow up with a warped conscience, or, if their conscience remains true, they learn to place no value on parental rebuke. In either case the result is bad. It may be very inconvenient to you to have your children's clothes spoiled, or your best china broken, but you have no right to treat such matters with the same gravity as you would acts of falsehood or selfishness. Let your children feel the evil consequences of their carelessness if you will; but keep your serious rebukes and moral indignation for serious moral offences. Treat small matters lightly, troublesome mistakes cheerfully, and reserve your grave reproaches for real sins. Only so will your censure be remembered and respected, and be really telling in its effect.

Society treats its members very much as some parents their children. It invents a number of conventional virtues and vices; and it rewards these conventional virtues and punishes these conventional vices, with higher rewards and severer penalties than it does those that belong to the divine order of things. Matters of etiquette are treated as if they were equally important with matters of real character; and a breach of manners is visited almost as severely as a breach of morals. A man, well-to-do in business, who lives in a fine house, will not have his character too closely scrutinized; but poverty, in the eyes of the world, is an unpardonable crime. Society mixes up matters of outward circumstance and inward character, superficial distinctions of rank and wealth and real distinctions of moral conduct, as though they were of equal importance, or sometimes even as though the mere social advantages were of the more importance of the two: and thus shows plainly the need of a truer spiritual perspective.

But truly great souls rise above this social narrowness and confusion. To them all things in life's picture assume their true proportions. In the foreground stand, prominent and clearly marked, essential matters of conduct, great principles, high truths, important duties; in the middle distance stand lesser duties and matters of smaller interest, and away in the shadowy background fall all those small and unessential things that are so often magnified in commoner souls. Such men and women grasp a clear conception of life. They are able to distinguish between the real and the conventional, between the great and the trivial. They are too intent on matters of real moment to quarrel about trifles. They see too clearly the supreme importance of moral distinctions to care overmuch about social conventionalisms. They are always ready to overlook the tithes of mint and anise and cummin, if only they can secure judgment, mercy and faith. Such people are as salt in the earth. It does us good to be with them. Looked at as they view it, we see the worth and earnestness and beauty of life. When they speak, our hearts burn within us by the way; and, though they may use no sanctimonious phrase, we feel the underlying religion which has its home in their hearts.

For, friends, it is chiefly religion which gives this true proportion and correct perspective to a man's view of life. You know that in a picture all the lines supposed to be perpendicular to the surface should meet in what is called the vanishing point. Religion fixes this vanishing point in life, and calls it love. Towards this point of love all the lines of a true life converge. There they meet and blend into one. And so to the truly Christian eye it is clear that there is really only one thing needful. All the commandments, all duty, all virtue, are briefly comprehended in this saying, "Thou shalt love thy neighbour as thyself," and "love is the fulfilling of the law." Once let a man lay hold of this greatest religious truth, or rather once let it lay hold of him and deepen in his heart into a fixed conviction, and it will at once give proportion and beauty to all his thought and life.

One thing further let us understand and remember. As the artist cannot rightly represent nature without a knowledge of perspective laws, so neither can the observer understand and interpret nature without their help. And in like manner we need the knowledge of a spiritual perspective not only to picture life rightly to our consciences, but also to interpret it. You walk along a straight road, and the hedges seem to meet ahead of you and to block your way. But you know that that is only a perspective illusion, and that in reality they run parallel all along. The sky above us seems to curve and bend into a mighty dome, touching the horizon on either hand. But we know that this is only an appearance; that, in fact, it stretches every way, uniform and unbent. Watching some sunset among the hills, we notice the slanting rays diverging in all directions like spokes in a golden wheel; and yet we know that they are really as parallel as the metals of a railroad. Or sometimes the clouds will arrange themselves in great fan-like masses, all apparently converging to some point on the horizon; and still we know that there is no convergence in reality at all. But, in all these matters, unless we had some knowledge of perspective, nature would deceive us.

Even so it is in some spiritual things. To the mourner, sitting in the shadow of bereavement, it sometimes seems as if the lines of love, parallel in this world, had their vanishing point in death. To the patriot, toiling for his country's good, it seems sometimes as though all the efforts of noble, just and upright men ended in disaster and defeat. To all who labour for the Kingdom of God it will appear now and again that the progress of truth and justice and humanity is going to disappear in the triumph of evil and wrong. Never fear! These are only appearances, the effect of our shortsighted mortal vision. In reality, loving hearts shall go on side by side for ever; truth and justice will never really bend one hair's breadth from their way; goodness shall triumph over evil, blessing shall vanquish cursing, right shall win the victory over wrong, and the Kingdom of God, so far from being extinguished in death or evil, shall pursue its mighty progress through all the ages of eternity.

II.

𝕮𝖍𝖊 𝕾𝖙𝖗𝖆𝖎𝖙 𝕲𝖆𝖙𝖊.

Enter ye in by the narrow gate; for wide is the gate and broad is the way that leadeth to destruction, and many be they that enter in thereby. For narrow is the gate and straitened the way that leadeth unto life, and few be they that find it.—MATT. vii., 13-14.

IT is very easy to read into Scripture texts ideas and preconceptions of one's own; much easier, probably, than to get out of them the meaning of the original speaker or writer. It is not surprising, therefore, to find that men with a Calvinistic theology firmly rooted in their minds, should see in these words which I have chosen, a clear statement from the lips of Jesus himself of the doctrine of predestination. The narrow gate and the way of life, the wide gate and the way of destruction; the many hastening along the broad, fatal road, the few alone urging their way along the strait and rugged path: in all this there seems to the Calvinist a plain indication of his picture of the future, of a handful redeemed, against millions destined to be lost; of a sparsely peopled heaven, and a densely crowded hell.

And yet, if you will put all preconceptions on one side, you will see that the real thought in Jesus' mind was not in the least like this. He had drawn a crowd of simple, ignorant but, many of them, earnest people round him; and he was not talking theology to them, or spinning out theological theories,—he was giving them a few plain rules for living, and telling them a few plain facts about life. He was not speaking of the state of the dead, of final salvation and final perdition; he was not saying anything about the future life at all. He was speaking of life here and now. And he told them, what every man, who has ever tried to live a high, noble life, knows to be true, that the way to such a life is narrow and the entrance strait, and that those who go in thereat are sadly few. He said nothing about one man being destined to sin, another to holiness. He simply stated, what I think we all know to be a spiritual fact, that it is very hard to do right and very easy to do wrong. The broad way and the wide gate are the pleasures and facilities of sin. The narrow way and the strait gate are the effort and self-denial imposed by Christian duty. And there is absolutely no other way into the highest life, no other way to the Kingdom of God, either on earth or in heaven or any where else (this is what he wanted to teach his hearers) than that which lies through the strait gate of strenuous effort and self-denying love. "You men and women," I can imagine him saying, "don't think that you can go on living as so many of you do, journeying along your easy, sinful ways, and hope to find peace and blessing at the end. Don't think that you can put everything right by offering a few sacrifices in the Temple, or attending to a set of outward observances. There is only one path to the life of God, the path of duty, self-sacrifice and love, and the entrance is narrow and the way is rough; but you must begin at the beginning and manfully perform the whole journey, if you mean to reach the heavenly goal and win the perfect blessing. Begin right, therefore; make a good start. Enter in at the strait gate. And do not be surprised to find yourselves with the few; for those that do right are few. The many choose the broader and easier path of selfishness and sin."

This was plain and, to some of his hearers no doubt, not very palatable doctrine. But it was sorely needed. The great stream of humanity was then rushing headlong down a course of moral carelessness and debauchery, ending in a sea of ruin and spiritual death, and it was only a very few who set themselves earnestly to climb the rugged heights of holiness. The world needed a teacher who should show it the one true way of life.

And is not this teaching still needed by the world to-day? Eighteen centuries have done a good deal for the moral and religious progress of humanity, and the world is a far holier and happier place than it was when Jesus first trod the Galilean hills. But sin and selfishness, and the spiritual ruin which follows them, still plentifully abound: and it is still only the minority who make a definite, prayerful choice of the strait gate, and strenuously toil along the narrow way. I look about me and I see here a young man, there a young woman, earnestly seeking out the strait gate of obedience to the will of God; here and there I see men and women of middle life toiling along the narrow upward path, their burdens falling from them as they go; and a few saintly souls I know, who, by a long life of steadfast effort, have surmounted all the difficulties and passed all the dangers of the way: and I see that already they have entered into life, and that the peace of God is theirs, and that the glory of heaven shines round them even here. But look round you at the general life of the great city in all its phases, and say if this is the common rule of existence. I fear the most hopeful of us must confess that ease and pleasure, self-seeking and self-indulgence are still fatal snares to the great majority of men, and that the broad, pleasant road, whose end is destruction, is still crowded with weak and thoughtless souls. And if you have any doubt whether destruction is really at the end of this road, you have only to trace the career of any man who follows it out. Take any youth who, entering by the broad gate of what seems at first sight harmless selfishness, saunters heedlessly on into regions of dissipation or greed; and note how at every moment his integrity and his purity slip away from him, and all that was sweet and lovable in his nature dissolves and melts away; and you will see that every step he takes is one of moral degradation, and brings him nearer to ruin both of body and soul. Such ruin stands before every man who gives himself up to the gratification of his own selfish pleasure and the temptations of the world. I do not say that he will necessarily go all the way to such ruin. Some gracious influence may overtake him, and induce him to retrace his steps. But I fear it is a fact now, as it was eighteen hundred years ago, that more people are to be found wandering in the broad seductive way that eventually leads to destruction, than struggling up the narrow and arduous path of life.

Now that is a sad statement to make; but I am not going to prophesy smooth things to you, when things are anything but smooth. I want you to face this unpleasant fact: and I think it will be good for us thoroughly to realize that the way to eternal life is neither a broad nor an easy one, but both narrow and steep; and that only they who earnestly strive and pray can find and keep the track. Robert Browning begins and ends his poem of Easter Day with the same thought, " How very hard it is to be a Christian." It is hard, at any rate at first; and the man who despises the difficulty of the task is pretty sure to fail in surmounting it. To do wrong is easy, to do right is irksome; and the consequence is that if we make no conscious resolve and no strenuous effort to become better, we are pretty sure to grow worse, and it is just this necessity for effort and exertion which has caused the Church to speak of life, in varying metaphor, as a pilgrimage, a race and a battle. There is no goal to be gained or victory to be won by those who trifle and dawdle on the way, or by half-hearted combatants. Downright earnestness alone is able to win the crown of life. Downright earnestness alone will enable us to stand nearer heaven a year hence than we stand to-day. O! Friends, it does seem to me, when I see so many youths and maidens, and strong men and women, giving almost their whole thought and energy to their pleasures or their money-making or the acquirement of some social accomplishment, and apparently caring so little for matters of eternal moment—it does seem to me that the world strangely fails to appreciate the real import and seriousness of life. Only by strong resolve can we hope to make any progress in the narrow way.

But the great point which Jesus tried to impress upon his hearers was the necessity of beginning right, making a right start, entering in at the right gate. So many people seem to think that the two ways of life, the narrow and the broad, the right and the wrong, run side by side, so that a man may journey pleasantly for half the distance down the wrong road, and then suddenly slip through the hedge, or take some short cut, into the right one. It is an utter mistake. The paths lie, not parallel, but in directly opposite directions: and if you choose the wrong one, there is no way for you to rectify your mistake save by retracing your steps. You will have to enter in at the strait gate after all. There are no short cuts into the Kingdom of God. When, therefore, a man imagines that he can spend half his life in selfishness or dishonesty or hardness of heart, and then put everything right in a moment by a sudden repentance or some act of religion, he is simply deceiving his own soul. The path of life will have to be trod from the very beginning : and we must all go in at one gate, that of obedience to the will of God. We must seek the Kingdom of God first therefore, and make our religious fidelity not the final, but the initial step, in our course.

And yet I doubt if this is the common way of regarding our religious obligations. There is an immense temptation, especially in the hurry and press and competition of modern life, to defer the use of our religious principles until after the struggle is over, and success has been gained, and religious scruples can no longer be an obstacle. We do not like to be hindered in our getting rich, or whatever else be our aim, by doubts as to whether this or that course is exactly the right one; we do not like to have to take a more difficult path when there is an easier one at hand; and so we remove our religion out of our way at the present moment and give it a place further on in life. You know in what manifold forms the temptation to postpone entering in at the strait gate comes to men,—the cases which occur daily, in the experience of every one of us, in which a man may act with more or less regard to truth and honesty, may be hard upon others and eager for self, may take an unfair advantage, may be a party to transactions of very doubtful character under the excuse of the rule of the trade, may pursue wealth or pleasure without overt sin, and yet hardly without moral guilt, may be utterly and irreligiously absorbed in worldly ends. I apprehend that a large number of those who give way to such temptations are by no means intentionally irreligious, but are simply deluding themselves with the thought that they can put off being religious until some future and more convenient opportunity. They will do wrong now to gain some advantage, and then atone for the wrong afterwards by making a good use of the advantage thus gained. They will gain by the wrong-doing now, and not lose by it in the end. There comes a time, perhaps, in a man's life, when some rare opportunity, some new speculation, some fresh channel, opens to him ; but it involves doing something to which his conscience will not quite agree. Shall he embrace the opportunity and pay no heed to his conscience ; or has he enough faith in God to forego it ? He accepts the world's doubtful offer, and he stills the inward monitor by assuring himself that, though he do this one wrong thing, yet, the crisis over, he will be a thoroughly good man ever afterwards. When once his fortune is made, there shall be no mistake about it. Then he will be a powerful supporter of every good work. But just now, in the thick of the struggle, now at the very crisis of his fortune, he must be allowed a little latitude, and religious principles must not be pressed home too severely. In fact religion must wait a little. He must go with the crowd down the broad road for a while, and then he will turn into the narrow path by and by.

Brethren, it cannot be done. You cannot gather grapes of thorns, or figs of thistles. A religious character is a natural growth, and needs a congenial soil ; and it is an absurdity to think that it will grow upon the soil of a worldly heart. There is no vainer thought than for a man to imagine that he can give the best part of his life to worldliness and then put in religion at the end. A religious character is produced by regular laws of cause and effect. It is the outcome of trial and temptation successfully wrestled with and overcome ; and to imagine that the trial may be dispensed with on the understanding that the man is going to be religious at some future date when there is no trial, is a gross superstition. What is the value of a man's goodness, who is ready to bear trial only when there is none to bear ? It is a mere outward profession. It is no living inward reality at all. Never, therefore, must we override our religious scruples, trusting to a future when we shall be able to wipe all wrongs away. Never must we do anything in the struggle of life, which we would not do afterwards. Never let us listen for one moment to the tempting suggestion that religion sets up too high a standard for the active practical part of life, but may be brought in at the close ; nor ever lay the flattering unction to our soul, that any good we can do with advantages wrongfully gained, can atone for the wrong committed in gaining them. Friends, I know not in what shape the temptation will come to you. But some temptation of this kind (to choose the Kingdom of God not first, but afterwards) presents itself, I believe, to every one of us. May God help you when it comes to say " Now is the time for firmness. Here the paths diverge; here is the parting of the ways. The choice cannot be postponed ; it must be made now. I will enter in at the strait gate."

Fellow worshippers, two ways of life are open before us ; the one a broad one—living for self ; the other a narrow one—living for humanity and God. The one destroys, the other leads to eternal life. All selfishness, every human pursuit and worldly influence, even the highest intellectual self-culture, if it ministers only to self-gratification, is soul-destroying. You may hang a man with a hempen or a silken cord : it is a halter still. So our self-seeking stifles the soul, whether it be pleasure or business, lust or care. On the other hand, all self-sacrifice ministers to the soul's life. It is even as it was said of old ; he that is willing to lose his life, shall truly find it. Surely then, we shall, one and all, resolve that we will not give ourselves just to the call and invitation of the present time, that we will not tread carelessly and thoughtlessly the downward path, simply because it is flowery and soft, and lies straight before us ; but that we will manfully seek out the strait gate and the narrow way, and give ourselves earnestly to that service of God which requires the genuine devotion of heart and soul and life.

> Life is real, life is earnest,
> And the grave is not our goal :
> " Dust thou art ; to dust returnest,"
> Was not spoken of the soul.

Therefore, let us remember through the days to come not only the things that are seen and temporal, but those also which are unseen and eternal.

III.

Self-Sacrifice.

For whosoever will save his life shall lose it ; and whosoever will lose his life for my sake shall find it.—MATT. xvi., 25.

This is one of those strange paradoxes in which great truths so often frame themselves. To one man it will seem utter nonsense; to another the statement of a grand spiritual fact. One will laugh it to scorn; another will cherish it as a holy secret. To some it will appear mere sentimentality; to others the very inmost law of life. It is one of those deep religious truths which seem to lie far down out of reach of our logic, high up above our purely intellectual grasp, right within and behind our external vision. It is the law of self-sacrifice—a law which can never be proved by arguments of utility, which you can hardly reduce to set forms, but which is nevertheless no spiritual absurdity, but a mighty spiritual truth. It is the one truth which Jesus taught, the one principle under which all his teaching came, the keynote of all his preaching. Other teachers before him saw it too, but only dimly; others, too, had struck the same note, but not with the same clear sound. Jesus proclaimed self-sacrifice as the essential factor of religion, the central idea of Christianity, the only expression of the Divine Life. It rings through all his words; it lives in all his deeds. We read it in all his life. It speaks to us from the cross as the very meaning of his death.

Self-sacrifice—what is it? It is the living in and for others, it is the spending and being spent for others; it is forgetting oneself and one's own interest, in concern for the welfare and interests of others; it is denying oneself to serve others; it is losing one's own life in the life of God and one's neighbour, and finding it there again larger, fuller and more real. It goes right in the teeth of all worldly wisdom. It frustrates the law of science whereby the weakest goes to the wall and the strongest survives. It upsets the calculations of the political economist, which are based on the assumption of every man for himself—universal self-interest. It is incomprehensible folly to the man of the world; but to those who have grasped it and practise it, it is the wisdom and power of God.

And in a most wonderful way the law of self-sacrifice comes true. You would think that the man who forgets and denies himself, lives not in his own life and thoughts, but in the lives and thoughts of others, would lose his own individuality. But is it so? Is it not rather a fact that it is just the men and women who have given themselves for others, and most denied themselves, who stand out with their individuality most strongly marked? You might think that the man who is always thinking about his own life and never troubling about the lives of those around him, would at any rate secure a strong individuality. But is it so? Is it not just these selfish, self-engrossed people, who never have any true individuality at all? Is it not a fact that he who wishes to save his life, loses it; and that he that loses his life most willingly, most certainly saves it?

Take the case of the hard, selfish, self-seeking man—the man who is always thinking about himself, always providing for himself, who makes self-enjoyment or self-education the end of his life. He lives among men, but not of them. All his looks are turned in upon himself. He is separated from his race by a hard shell of suspicion and distrust. His pulse never beats with the great pulse of humanity; the joys and sorrows of the world are scarcely reflected, never felt, in his soul. Anything that clashes with his own advancement, pleasure, culture, or refinement, he will have nothing to do with. He lives in and for himself. And what is the end of it? He lives alone and dies alone; and in his seeming life there is actual death. He loves his life and loses it.

And compare with this the life of Jesus, a life in which you can find no thought of self from one end to the other, a life wholly given to his fellow-men. What picture can be more sublime than the wonderful self-surrender and self-sacrifice of the sacred story? Not a thought of his own interest, or glory, or success; his whole being poured forth

into the trials and sorrows and sins of his people. To every
guilty or tear-stained soul with whom he spoke, he gave the
whole sympathy of his nature; forgot himself entirely in
entering into the sorrows and temptations of his brother's or
sister's life. From the beginning of his ministry until the
last great act of self-sacrifice upon the cross, we see him
continually pouring forth his life for others. And yet was
his life any the poorer because it was so freely given away?
On the contrary, there is no life which stands out so clearly
in all history, no individuality which is so strongly and distinctly marked. Jesus lived absolutely in and for others;
and yet I know of no personality so unique as his. No man
ever so lived in others. No man was ever so truly himself.
And the same thing is seen in Paul, Jesus' greatest follower.
He surrendered himself utterly to the mastery of Christ's
spirit. In the might of that spirit he accomplished his
work. In that work he was eager to spend and be spent.
The self-sacrifice of his life was most unconditional. Even
his own soul he was willing to lose, if his kinsmen might be
saved. He lived in and for his Master and his work. And
yet look, how sharp are the lines of his personality! See how
his character stands out in the history of the Church. He
entered into the life of Jew and Gentile, Greek and Roman;
he became all things to all men. He lost his own life in the
life of those he loved. And yet where, save in Jesus, will
you find so rich and full and true a life; where will you find
a character which has won and still retains an influence like
his? It was by losing his life that he saved it.

But may we not appeal to our own experience for evidence
of this truth? When has our life seemed truest and richest?
When has our being thrilled with the deepest intensity?
When have we known ourselves most thoroughly, and
realised the best that is in us? Has it not been in the hour
of self-denial, when we have given up some selfish pleasure
for a holy duty, when we have resigned some cherished plan
that we may help a brother on his way, when we have sacri-
ficed our lower self that we may be true to Christ and God?
Is there one of us who has not felt that just when he has
given up something of his own life to enrich the life of
another, just when in the fulness of love he is living in

others and has lost his own life in theirs, he has at that very moment found a higher and truer life, and known something of what is meant by living in God? Is it not universally true that the more we lose our own thoughts and feelings and interests, and the more we think and feel and plan for others, the richer, the fuller, the deeper does our own existence become?

This law of self-sacrifice, brethren, is the great central principle of Christianity. All the noble, self-denying work that is being done to-day to help the weakness and lessen the evil of the world is just Christianity acted out. When you see true men and women sacrificing their own ease, giving up something of their own lives, to teach the ignorant, to care for the criminal, to rescue the waifs and strays of the world—when you see them nursing the sick, softening the sufferings of the poor, strengthening them against their temptations, striving to conquer drunkenness, showing the way to better and happier modes of life,—you may be sure that the true spirit of Christ is in their hearts, and is the inspiration which sends them on their way. And when now and again you get a glimpse of that harder self-sacrifice, which is more seldom seen, but is often deeper and holier, the self-sacrifice which has to be made within the home-life and which most surely consecrates it, you may know that there is there the same strong love which enabled Jesus to endure the cross and despise the shame. If ever I feel inclined to think that the power of Christianity over men's hearts is growing weak, it is not when I hear men refuse to take the Christian name, it is not when I see them forsake the churches; it is when I see them shrinking from all self-sacrifice; because I know that then the spirit of Christ is not in their hearts. There is nothing to me so sad as to mark how many young men and young women to-day are living entirely self-engrossed lives—some caring only for their own comfort and ease, seeing the world's sin and sorrow, hearing " the still sad music of humanity," and yet touched with no strong sympathy, moved by no loving desire to share and help it, unwilling to deny themselves any pleasure or worldly advantage to help in bearing the general cross, and lightening the general burden; others caught in the smaller meshes of a more refined selfishness—the selfishness which leads them to take no thought save for their own self-improvement and self-education, and to decline, both in the home and in the world, every act of self-denial for which they can see no paying return. It is here that the power of Christ is dead; for where there is no self-sacrifice, there is no Christianity. They love their life, and they lose it.

There is a fine old Roman legend which narrates how St. Peter, on the night before his martyrdom in one of the terrible Roman persecutions, yielded to his own fears and the urgent desire of his fellow-Christians, and fled in terror from the city; how in the early dawn of morning he met Jesus walking towards the city with naked-bleeding feet and stayed him with the question, "Lord, whither goest thou?" He received the answer, with the awful look from the eyes of Christ, which he once before had met, "I go to Rome to be crucified again in thy stead." The apostle bowed his head in shame, took courage, returned, and witnessed a good confession. The legend is for many days. As often as we decline our cross, as often as we refuse to give up something of our life for others, as often as we turn away from the cup of self-denial which God holds out to us, so often do we put our Master to shame, deny the Christ and crucify him afresh. Would that in these moments of weakness we could have clearly presented to us the vision of the crucified, could meet his reproachful yet loving eyes, could hear his gentle voice, could see his wounded feet; and so, realizing all the might of his great self sacrifice, could find the strength to bear our crosses too! What we need in order to alter all our selfishness is the spirit of Jesus Christ.

And, brethren, when we have gained the willing spirit, when we are ready to give up something of our own lives, we must beware of looking for too great opportunities for the exercise of our self-denial. It is only a few of us who are called upon to perform acts of great self-sacrifice. But we are all asked to do those little daily acts of love which grace a Christian life. It is not so much the nerving of ourselves to do great deeds of self-renunciation that is required, as the constant habit of merging our own lives in the lives of others, throwing ourselves out of ourselves in wide and tender sympathy, living for others, and not for ourselves. There is no small danger that if we are always watching for great opportunities of doing service for God, we may miss the chances which every day brings with it of pouring forth our lesser lives in little acts of self-forgetful love and helpful sympathy, and finding the larger life which is lived in God. Let me illustrate this by quoting another legend. It tells us how, when men's hearts were first kindled by the thought that the Lord's enemies possessed the holy places where he had lived and died, a band of religious knights set forth to seek for and recover the Holy Grail, the cup into which Christ had poured the wine at the last supper. It tells us how one of these, after long and fruitless search, came back, worn out and grey, to find another established in his home. And now in the cold winter time he sat without his own barred gate, dreaming of the light and warmth of the sunnier lands from which he had just returned. Suddenly he was startled by seeing close beside him the loathsome form of a leper, who begged from him an alms. In deep humility the knight remembered the old pride with which, as he first set forth upon his search, he had thrown an alms to a leper, who then, as now, stood before his gate. He parted in twain the single crust that remained to him, he broke the ice of the stream that flowed by him, and he gave the leper to eat and to drink. Then he looked up and lo! not the leper but the Lord Christ himself stood before him—

> And the Voice that was calmer than silence said,
> ' Lo, it is I, be not afraid!
> In many climes without avail,
> Thou hast spent thy life for the Holy Grail;
> Behold it is here,—this cup that thou
> Didst fill at the streamlet for me but now;
> This crust is my body broken for thee,
> This water his blood that died on the tree;
> The Holy Supper is kept indeed,
> In whatso' we share with another's need,—
> Not that which we give, but what we share,—
> For the gift without the giver is bare;
> Who bestows himself with his alms, feeds three,
> Himself, his hungering neighbour, and me.'

And so we, too, may most often find the Christ we seek

at our very doors. The Holy Grail, the symbol of the fuller Christly life, is after all just our daily life and our common work sanctified and transfigured by the spirit of self-sacrifice. That is the spirit which Jesus lived and died to make manifest. That is the spirit which the world is still waiting for to-day. For when the world has grasped it and learnt it, the world will be saved, and the Kingdom of God will have come.

IV.
Modern "Seeking after a Sign."

And when the people were gathered thick together, he began to say: This is an evil generation: they seek a sign; and there shall no sign be given it, but the sign of Jonas the prophet.—LUKE xi., 29.

I SUPPOSE that the world has never been entirely free from the low unspiritual craving for signs and wonders. Certainly it was not free from that craving at the time when Jesus appeared upon the scene. On the contrary, the Jews were untiring in their search for the marvellous, and no religious teacher could hope to win any large hearing unless he could guarantee his teaching by some sensational miracle. The people always wanted external proofs for spiritual things, demanded for every inward revelation that it should be accredited by some outward sign, and preferred to enter the Temple of Religion through the gate of the senses and under the guidance of wonder, rather than through the gate of the Spirit and under the guidance of faith. One of the first great temptations, therefore, which met the new teacher was the temptation to yield to this passion of the age, and to employ his powers for the sake of winning the favour of the multitude, and in the attempt to establish the kingdom of God by other than the highest means. Jesus conquered that temptation; and his victory is figured forth for us in the story of the Satanic prompting to fling himself down from a pinnacle of the Temple. He saw that however leadership and sects may be established, the Kingdom of God must follow the slow and orderly unfolding of spiritual life—first the blade, then the ear, then the full corn in the ear, and that no appeal to the senses could really touch the inner man; and so he turned a deaf ear to the seductive voice, and declared that no sign would he give. But the sign-seeking spirit of the world proved a hindrance and an obstacle to him throughout his career,—even mocking him upon the cross, with " If he be indeed the king of Israel let him now come down from the cross and we will believe him;" as though any outward sign would secure the faith of men who were blind to that wonder of love and self-devotion which was exhibited before their eyes on Calvary. But Jesus never faltered. His greatest utterances were all spoken in a spirit directly contrary to this religion of the senses. He turned men to the witness of their own hearts. He swept away all the jugglery of superstitious ceremonial with which men had overlaid the simple thought of God. He called them back to a more natural life and feeling, a simpler and purer morality, a more child-like trust in a Father ever loving and ever near. God, to him, was not the wonder-worker of the Jews, but a Spirit, demanding a spiritual worship, arising out of a deep feeling of spiritual need: "God is a Spirit; and they that worship him must worship him in spirit and in truth." It was all too high, too simple, too spiritual for the Jewish taste. They wanted a sign. Christ would not pander to their unspiritual craving. Hence the answer, stern and strong: An evil and adulterous generation seeketh after a sign. There shall no sign be given it, save that of Jonas the prophet,—that is to say, simply a preaching of the truth.

Well, the world then was not very unlike the world now, and signs and wonders are still in great request in our modern Christian society. Let us consider, to-day, our need of a finer and loftier spirituality.

This need is really of a part with the general tendency of the age to run after whatever is flashy, exciting, brilliant, or marvellous—however superficial it may be, in preference to what is real, solid and deep. It is a tendency pretty obvious ; but if you want an example, look how it is reflected in our literature. People to-day want brilliant, showy, or startling writing ; otherwise, they will have nothing to say to it. Unless they read signs and wonders they will not read at all. Books that excite the imagination, without giving too much trouble to the reader's power of thought ; articles written in a sparkling style, and flavoured with a spice of sensation ; writing that keeps the reader's attention by a series of surprises or wonders,—this is the kind of food most relished by the intellectual palate of the age : and anything which cannot show for itself these outward signs, stands very little chance of being at all widely read. The consequence is, that, while a few thoughtful men, who are strong of purpose and careless of what the world thinks or says, persist in writing books of worth and weight; the majority drift into mere sensationalists, prostitute the higher gifts of their genius, write merely for the season, strain after startling or dazzling effects in order to catch the popular ear, and so fall into the very temptation which Christ successfully resisted. And the consequence to society is that, tainted with a diseased craving for this frothy sensational class of writing, men find a constant and increasing difficulty in reaching that temper of mind which is needed to comprehend the unsensational life of Jesus Christ. For that life is equally unsatisfying to the sign-seeking Jew of old, and the sign-seeking Englishman of to-day. It offers no sign to either of them. Apart from its moral and spiritual glory, it was a quiet and common life enough. Uneventful save in its close, void of all sensation, natural, unartificial, cool, quiet, deep—no man can understand it, no man can understand Jesus himself, no man can understand the profound simplicity and spirituality of his teachings, if he has accustomed himself to a long course of mental stimulants, in his thirst for morbid excitement. This may not seem to you a very important matter, but considered in all its bearings it is really a very considerable evil. This taste for sensational literature is in fact corrupting men's hearts, and, further, is merely one indication of a wide-spread tendency, which constitutes our people of to-day, like the Jews of eighteen hundred years ago, "an evil generation that seeketh for a sign."

See how this tendency shows itself in matters of religion. Which are the churches that most easily win the popular ear, that draw the greatest crowds within their gates, that are most attractive to the average English mind? Are they the most spiritual churches; the churches that are truest in their methods and teachings to the high spirituality of their Master? By no means. They are the churches that are readiest to yield to the demand for signs and wonders, that are the most willing to stoop from the spirit of Christ to the spirit of the world, that make the largest bid in mere materialistic excitements and attractions. Look at the constant endeavour that is made to awaken religious sensibility by the overwrought fervour of the revivalist, producing a morbid and hysterical excitement which is mistaken for spiritual activity, but which is really quite a different thing. Or look at the efforts put forth to produce a spiritual result by means of the sensual impressions made by the lights, incense, vestures and all the other paraphernalia of the ritualists. I do not deny that revivalists have succeeded in producing a certain amount of real enthusiasm, and in doing a certain amount of real good. I do not deny the real enthusiasm produced and the real good done by the efforts of the ritualists. Where good men are at work good results will ensue, however mistaken their methods. But what I do complain of is this—that revivalist and ritualist alike, to a certain degree, both try to produce spirituality from without, both stoop from the high methods of Christ, both pander to the popular craving for signs, both make use of stimulants which however well adapted to produce a physical excitement are entirely unnatural in relation to the soul. Both, it seems to me, yield to the temptation which Christ conquered, and which his Church ought to conquer too—the temptation to promote the welfare of the Church and Kingdom of God by the employment of unworthy and merely sensational means.

The same evil is apparent again in that large class of persons who hunt after exciting sermons. The only difference is that they seek an intellectual rather than a sensual sign. There is a large and, I am afraid, an increasing number of people, with whom worship has degenerated into that far lower thing, going to hear a certain preacher, who are always on the look-out for an intellectual treat, who like to have their imagination tickled by the discussion of curious and fanciful subjects, and who are more disappointed than they can tell, when they hear only what they call "an ordinary religious sermon." Like the ancient Athenians, they spend their time in seeking "some new thing," and have no liking for those great gospel truths which are common as the sunshine and eternal as God. They fancy that they can repair the ravages of six days' worldliness by merely listening to an eloquent sermon; they mistake intellectual excitement for spiritual conviction; and they go to church to be pleased with the preaching rather than to win the power to conquer evil. This is merely a modern form of the old seeking after signs. I should be glad to think that many of these sermon-hunters get much good from what they hear. But I am forced to believe that such is the case with very few of them. I have known a good many of these greedy devourers of preaching. You may see them drinking in the words of any notable preacher. If there is any thought, stir, or cleverness in the preaching, their sensibilities ripple into an ecstasy of quiet delight. But I can never find that the effect goes much further. As a rule they are not people of strong, well-disciplined spiritual life. They receive a certain grateful stimulus, an entertainment of the intellectual faculties, and there the matter ends. Nay, even though they listen to a Martineau, a Manning, or a Liddon, they remain very much the same kind of men that they were before; they are like St. James's "hearer of the word," they go their way, and straightway forget what manner of men they are; or, even worse, they come to mistake their cultivated facility for intellectual and emotional excitement for real spiritual power and actual progress in noble living. So it must always be, to some extent, with those who frequent the churches seeking for signs, instead of that silent unseen strength that comes from a spiritual communion with God.

Take, again, as another indication of the survival amongst us of the Jewish passion for signs and wonders which Jesus so warmly denounced, the existence in the present day of a strong craving for a false and materialistic form of the supernatural. What is our modern so-called "Spiritualism" but the old asking for a sign? I know that this is debatable ground, and that some of you may differ from me very widely in your estimate of the Spiritualistic movement. So be it. If you can find in it any genuine spiritual light and help, by all means accept them. To me, judged simply by what one can see and read about it, and regarded in its whole tendency, it appears to be about as unspiritual a movement as one can possibly imagine; for whatever may be the case in exceptional instances, the general effect is to attract people and fascinate them not with the purely spiritual, but with the outwardly marvellous, with the manifestation of things which astonish the senses rather than of those which ennoble the soul. And therefore I hold that its general tendency is bad. People sit round tables, have things told them or see manifestations of force which they cannot explain, listen to speeches made in trance, and fancy that this is in some way spiritual and religious. But it is not necessarily so at all. For my part, I am quite willing to believe that there may possibly be forces developed at some of these circles, which are as yet unexplained, and which have a certain interest as problems of science; but I have not one particle of faith that these forces, or any fact or word that I ever read or heard of in connection with spiritualism, ever came from the world of spirits. But even supposing they did, that would not make them spiritual. A spiritual communication is one that opens my soul to the divine life, and uplifts me in the grade of truth, feeling, aspiration and love. If any being can make me see something of the divineness of goodness, of the all-penetrating grace of heaven, of the beauty of holiness, can touch my soul to its depths and uplift me to a higher plane of feeling and to clearer views of the worth and meaning of life—then I get a spiritual communication, and it makes no difference to its spirituality whether I get it through a medium, or from my next-door neighbour, or from the page of some printed book. But if an angel should come to me to-night and talk a little gossip, and then go away;—well, I should have seen the figure of an angel, and that would be all. I should have had no spiritual communication whatever. And hence my chief objection to spiritualism. As far as I can see it is not spiritual. Its machinery is materialistic, and its matter is gossip and commonplace. For my part I do not care in the least to talk to a bore and a simpleton just because he has no bones and flesh. If he can reveal to me any spiritual truth, if he can give me any higher ideas of God and duty, than I can get already from the songs of the Psalmist and the words and life of Jesus Christ—then I will listen to him; but not otherwise. And I am convinced that in this respect, that is to say in real spiritual elements, spiritualism can give us nothing that is not starved and poor compared with what we already have access to here. If I want to get into spiritual communion with Shakespeare or Theodore Parker, surely I shall do so far better by studying Hamlet and the Discourse of Religion, than I shall by listening to the weak drivel that mediums profess to extract from these men's ghosts. And surely if I want to know anything about God and duty and the divine life, I shall do better to seek it on my knees in prayer than through any materialistic knockings and rappings. For spiritual things must be spiritually discerned. The whole question of the worth of spiritualism—quite apart from that of its truth—is dependent on a clear conception of what is spiritual and what is not. As long as people think that details about the life of the departed, and the way they spend their time, and how near they are to us physically, are spiritual matters; so long, I suppose, they will think it worth while holding séances and employing mediums.

Have you ever thought how majestically silent the Bible is in the matter of gossip about the world to come? All through the Old Testament there is not a word about the details of the spirit life. The great spiritual passages are all about the providence of God, the evil of sin and the blessedness of obedience. The New Testament is equally silent. Not in a single sentence does Jesus ever stoop to human curiosity about the in-door life of heaven. He talks almost unceasingly about a kingdom of heaven that is to have rule in men's hearts. Paul says he was caught up to heaven in a trance; but I don't know that he ever claimed to be a medium; his spirituality was really in his deep sense of God's nearness and love. Even the Book of Revelation is not an unveiling of heaven; but simply a picture in symbols of an expected kingdom on earth. All through the New Testament you will find the conviction that inward states—not outward tidings—are the only possible media of communion with God.

That is the true, and, as it seems to me, the only reverent, spirit. The veil that hides the life beyond the grave is not intended to be lifted. For sure am I that if God had meant us to know anything of what is going on on the further side, he would have chosen some worthier means of communication than is afforded by a modern séance. But, brethren, we can have communion with the spiritual world: for that world is here as well as there. As Christians, as children of God, we are bound to pray and strive for such communion. It comes to us in every new insight we gain into the nature of the universe, whereby we see the quickening life and love of God throbbing in all the world about us. It comes to us in seasons of silence, when we cleanse the windows of our souls for the inpouring of the divine light. It comes to us in all prayer for heavenly guidance, in all consecration to the work and will of God. Most of all it comes to us, when in the spirit of Christ, we go out into the world and do our duty against the evil. There, brethren, in the world's great contest, the strife between moral light and darkness, happiness and misery, holiness and sin; there, fighting the good fight of faith and bearing a noble part, you will gain some real knowledge of spiritual things. You want to put yourself into communion with the holy dead? Then tread in their footsteps, take up their work; endure, like them, all things for the truth. You want inspiration? Seek out some self-sacrificing labour and you shall be inspired by God's own breath of life. You need excitement? Throw yourself into the warfare against sin within and wrong without, enter the lists with your own temptations, match yourself against some demon of the world, and you shall find an excitement that is good for you and an enthusiasm that will not flag. It is not through séances, it is not by asking for signs, that you will find access to the spiritual world. You must go forth into life, and seek it through loving labour and faithful prayer. And there, depend upon it, in the arena of life, where the gentlest charities are found and the noblest victories are won, you will rise into fellowship with the Infinite Spirit of the Universe, and feel the presence of God himself in your hearts.

Oh, that the world would grow up to this more spiritual ideal, that it would cease to run after sensations and wonders, and ask for signs no more; that it would leave the methods of revivalist and ritualist and spiritualist all behind for ever, and come to seek and worship God who is a Spirit, in spirit and in truth! To that end at least let us strive and work and pray.

V.

"I will follow thee, but"—

And another also said, Lord, I will follow thee; but let me first go bid them farewell, which are at home at my house. And Jesus said unto him, No man, having put his hand to the plough and looking back, is fit for the kingdom of God.—LUKE IX., 61, 62.

AT first sight that seems a hard saying. The man's request was such a harmless one that one would think it might reasonably have been granted. But Jesus' refusal was not so unreasonable as it appears to be on the face of it. We must take into consideration the object which he had in view. He was on the look-out for men of the right sort to help him in his great work. He did not care so much that they should exactly comprehend what that work was, what its precise scope and significance, as that they should be animated by a spirit of complete loyalty and allegiance, and of perfect confidence in him as their guide and teacher. He wanted men of brave, ready, unhesitating mind, such as alone would fit them for the lives they would have to live, and the work they would have to do. And so he invented a somewhat strange, and, at first sight, unreasonably exacting, but in reality a very shrewd and searching, test. Whatever they might be doing, whatever difficulties might seem to stand in the way, he asked them at once to leave all and to follow him, to follow him without hesitation and without conditions. And so he discovered whether they did really trust him from the bottom of their hearts, or not. Let us take two scenes to illustrate how this trial worked.

By the lake-side at Capernaum was a custom-house, where the tolls were collected on the goods and produce brought across the lake. The publican, the man who farmed the taxes from the Roman Government, was a Jew, named Matthew. He had often seen Jesus, had watched him pass with his little knot of disciples, and now and then had listened to what he was saying. At first he regarded this new teacher with a mere feeling of curiosity, but soon a deeper interest was awakened, and by and bye he felt a strange power taking hold of his heart, and he began to love and to trust him. Jesus, I have no doubt, perceived something of what was going on in Matthew's mind; and so one day as he sat taking the tolls, Jesus abruptly bade him to rise and follow him. He did this at a most inconvenient time, just when the man was busiest, and Matthew might have found twenty excuses, and right good ones too, for postponing his compliance until a more suitable season. But he employed none of them. Unexpected as it was, he felt that here was a call that might not be repeated, an opportunity that he might never have again, and so at Jesus' summons, so the story briefly puts it, he left all, and arose, and followed him. That is one picture —a picture of implicit and unhesitating obedience.

Let us look again. It is by the same sea-side, and the shades of evening are falling on the hills and closing in over the waters, as Jesus is preparing to embark upon the lake. He has been talking to the people, and great crowds have been listening to his words, but now the multitudes have gone, and only a few linger in his gracious presence, unable to tear themselves away. How deep does their discipleship go? Is it perfect and entire, wanting nothing? Or does it lack something yet? A scribe steps forward from the group, and in a moment of strong enthusiasm, declares " Master, I will follow thee whithersoever thou goest." Jesus neither accepts nor repels the proffered allegiance; but, pointing over the waves to the darkening sky, replies " Foxes have holes, and the birds of the air have nests, but the Son of Man hath not where to lay his head." It was quite enough. The man's resolution oozes away, and we hear of him no more. Then Jesus addresses himself directly to two others standing near, who seemed most drawn to him of all, and tells them to follow him. A minute ago, and, I daresay, they had both been longing to become his disciples and be with him always. But this is a little sudden. Cannot the summons be postponed? The one has just lost his father, and would like to complete the long funeral solemnities. After they are over, then he will come. But now, this minute? No, he cannot follow Jesus just now. The other also would like to join the little band of disciples, but to do it to-night he feels is somewhat too precipitate. He will go and talk it over first with his friends, and come to-morrow or the next day. Lord, I will follow thee, he protests, but not now,—let me first go bid farewell to them which are at home at my house. And so they missed the flood-tide of their destiny, and henceforth all their life must be bound in shallows. "But," you say, "the reasons they gave were very good ones." So they were; excellent, admirable, reasons. Only here is the fact— they had a chance of following Jesus, and they did not take it. The call came, and was not accepted. The door of opportunity opened for a brief moment, and they went not in. They hesitated, they hung back—the golden moment passed and came no more; Jesus went his way and they went theirs. I don't exactly blame them. I daresay they lived afterwards good, respectable lives, as things go. Only they might have been apostles. They might have trod the grandest path ever given to men to tread. And I think of all they missed.

The story is (to my mind) a very suggestive one, because it exactly typifies so much of our religion to-day. "Lord, I will follow thee, but—." That is just what the Christianity of a good many of us amounts to. We reverence Christ, we desire to be his true disciples, but we fail when it comes to the point. We just miss the truest discipleship because we will put in that qualifying "but." We have a real, genuine love for Jesus, a real longing to make ourselves his faithful followers; yet, in spite of this longing and this love, we constantly hesitate and hang back when our Christianity is put to the test—we constantly just fall short of a hearty and thorough discipleship. Let us look into this a little more closely.

I say that multitudes have a real, genuine love for Jesus. I believe if you could read men's hearts clearly, you would find in most of them a sincere and honest wish to live a Christian life. I believe that the cry, "Lord, I will follow thee," expresses what is really at the bottom of our souls. Some people think that the world's religion is mostly a sham. They point to the large professions of Christianity and the small performance of it, and they say, "See what a piece of hypocrisy it all is. Men talk very loudly about their allegiance to Christ, but how much better are their lives in consequence? Who honestly tries to obey him? Who genuinely attempts to live by his example?" But such condemnation, though easily passed, is not altogether deserved. Of course there is a certain amount of truth in it. No doubt religion is in some cases purely put on, assumed purely for fashionable purposes. But not, I think, at all commonly so. On the whole, the reverence paid to Christ and Christianity comes, I believe, of a deep and real conviction that Jesus is our true leader, and that he really can show us the way of life, as none else can, if only we have faith enough, and trust enough, and courage enough, to follow him. I know that it is hard to reconcile men's conduct with their creed, difficult to harmonise the folly and sin and worldliness of society with its constant profession of religious faith. But however little it may come to the surface, I believe that deep down in men's hearts, almost buried sometimes amid the rubbish of frivolity and sin, there is mostly a sincere desire to walk in the way of Christ, and to be a Christian cost what it may. If we could see men as they really are at their centre, we should find, I am persuaded, that Christ has a very strong hold upon the heart of the world.

Now, I don't think we recognise this quite as fully as we should. We see the selfishness and the wickedness of the world, and we are apt to conclude that people do wrong because they have no desire to do right, that they live unchristian lives because they have realised no strong call to live Christian lives; and so we go to work to demonstrate to them the superiority of right-doing over wrong-doing, and the exceeding beauty of a Christ-like character. But, as a rule, that is not what they need. They know that it is better to do right than to do wrong, as well as you do. Very likely they admire a Christian life as much as you do. And they are not in the least enamoured of their own sins. They have got the right desire somewhere in their hearts, only they fail in giving it effect. They lack the strength of will to carry it out. And what they need is not so much showing that Christ is worth following, as being helped and encouraged and strengthened to follow him when the call actually comes. The drunkard knows perfectly well that he is a fool to drink, sees perfectly clearly the higher sanctity of a temperate life, and it is of very little use your either telling him that he is a fool, or pointing out to him the advantages of temperance. The poor wretch has learnt all that by a bitter experience. All you can do for him is to help him to follow his own knowledge and his own inmost desire, rather than the outward temptation, when the moment of trial comes. You have got to strengthen his will, not to change his mind. And I think that, generally, we should better help the sinning humanity around us if we did not quite so readily assume that higher aims and longings are absent from the sinner's heart; if we were quicker to see that, as a rule, there is the perfectly genuine wish, "Lord, I will follow thee," but that the man is not morally strong enough to act up to his own best desires.

And so in the case of our own lives. Let us recognise the real love of God and Christ and goodness that is in our hearts, and the genuine desire we have to live a Christ-like life. Let us not despair of our religion and think our faith worthless because it seems sometimes to have so little effect. It is good as far as it goes—real as far as it goes—only, unfortunately, it does not always go far enough to secure complete control over the conduct of our lives.

But if men's intentions are generally right, whence, you may ask, the so constant failure in their performance? Well, I believe it arises simply from the fact that we will not bring ourselves, whenever we feel a higher leading or hear a diviner call, to yield a prompt and ready obedience. The thought of Christianity, the prompting to live an unselfish, pure, Christ-like life, comes to us to-day, just as the actual call of Jesus came to the men of old, and, instead of obeying at once, taking the higher path there and then, we begin to make excuses and to postpone our obedience. We feel we ought to obey—we hear and understand the call; but it always seems to come at an inconvenient time, or to necessitate our giving up something which we especially wish not to give up; and so we hesitate and beg for a little delay. We will follow the higher leading to-morrow, next week, next month, next year; but we must just finish what we are doing to-day. We do really want to be Christians by and bye, but we cannot give up being heathens just now.

We say "Lord, we will follow thee, but"—first let us do something else.

In the Confessions of St. Augustine, whose early life was anything but saintly, he relates how in his youth he had prayed to God and begged chastity of Him, saying "Give me chastity and continency—only not yet." There is something very human about that prayer. It corresponds very closely to a good deal of our praying to-day. Here, for instance, is a young man, living an average life better, according to the world's standard, than Augustine's, but neither very virtuous nor very vicious. He is enjoying the hey-day of his youth, thinking a good deal about his pleasure and his position in life, and thinking a little also, though not very much, about religion. And some day there comes to him, as there comes to us all, a sense that something more is required of him, a sense that there is a deeper, larger, holier life to be lived than the one he is leading, a feeling of the deeper realities of life and a call to a higher and truer service. In how many cases does not the young man's answer take shape somewhat after this fashion? "Lord, I will follow thee, I will seek this truer service, I will rise to this holier life; only not yet. I mean to do high and worthy things some day, but there is time enough for these more serious matters by and bye. Just now I want to remain a little as I am." He hesitates, and he is lost.

Or, again, perhaps this vision of a Christian life, this sense of its high worth and power and peace, comes to us amid the busy cares of our manhood and womanhood—comes to us as an invisible Christ, and stands at our door and knocks. We know who it is. We recognise the call. Our hearts long to arise and follow and obey. But then, we say, how can we, situated just as we are? How can a man be a Christian after any very noble fashion, when he has his way to make in a hard, unscrupulous world? How can I follow Christ with perfect loyalty, involved, as I am, in this fierce struggle and competition of life? No, I will follow faithfully by and bye, but I must go on as I am going now a little while longer, until I am more independent of the ways and customs of the world. Ah! how deep in human nature lies the thought that a man may do a little wrong now, and then

atone for it afterwards by the good use he will make of the
advantages gained. There comes some trying moment in a
man's life, when the world offers great things, if only he will
deviate a little from the right and true path. The man
knows that the really Christ-like thing to do is to forego the
world's offer. But he cannot quite bring his mind to that,
and so he makes a compromise with himself. He will adopt
the lower course now, but he will be a thoroughly good man
afterwards. First of all, he says, let me make my fortune.
Then, afterwards, when my position is established, I will do
a great deal of good through my wealth and my power.
Religion shall be no loser in the end. I shall be able to
fight Christ's battles in the world all the more effectually
by and bye. But first I must make my way in life secure.
And so the day for following Christ is postponed. People
persuade themselves that religion can wait a little, that it is
not suitable to the present crisis; that now in the very thick
of the struggle, they must be allowed a little liberty, but
that afterwards, please God, it shall be different. It is the
old story, "Lord, I will follow thee, but"—

And so it constantly happens that we wait to give ourselves
to God, until we have nothing left but the dregs of our life
to bring to Him. We live for the world and the things of
the world, as long as we can get anything out of them, and
then we come to religion when the world casts us off and
will give us no more. Men come to God in their old age,
their sorrow, their desolation. They did not come in their
youth, their prosperity and their joy. They come to lay the
poor worn-out fragments of their life upon the altar on
which they ought to have laid their best and earliest fruits.
In life's morning they take no heed of the divine invitation.
They turn to God only when all else has failed. Oh, what a
poor, mean, ungrateful response to God's rich love and
neverfailing mercies!

Now, friends, let us be on our guard in all these matters.
Whether the summons to follow Christ comes to us in the
matter of raising the whole character of our life, or whether
we are simply asked to do some hard duty, to give up some
cherished plan, to make some particular self-sacrifice, let us
remember that the time to show our discipleship is at the

moment when it is put to the test. Christianity comes to men to-day, just as Jesus himself came in the olden time, and always asks us to give up something which just at that moment seems hardest and most inconvenient to give. You can find plenty of excuses, if you like, for not complying with the demand—good valid reasons which no one can find fault with, and which will possibly completely quiet your own conscience. Only remember this: Christ will have asked something of you, and you will have refused it; will have invited you, and you will have hung back; will have bidden you follow him, and you will have gone your own way instead. You will have missed that prompt ready discipleship, which, at the Master's voice, leaves all and follows him, and having put the hand to the plough, never for one moment looks back.

But it is only fair to say that we have, in all this, matter for our regret rather than for our censure. It is not an easy thing to follow Christ, and I do not think that in those old gospel times Jesus felt either anger or contempt for those who shrank from following him. When he put that hard condition upon the rich young ruler, and the young man went sorrowfully away, I do not think Jesus loved him one bit the less. Only I can imagine what a yearning sorrow and disappointment must have filled his heart, that men should choose the ordinary common way, when he would have led them by high and glorious paths to a peace and joy unspeakable. May it not be that he is looking with some such feeling on our lives to-day, rejoicing at the true love and reverence that is in our hearts, sorrowing that so often we hesitate and hang back, and postpone our obedience, that so seldom we follow him fearlessly and without delay? And would it not be a great and happy thing for us if we had a stronger, heartier, readier faith—if we could always feel that our religion is for present, and not for future, use, so that at every call of Christ or duty, we should make no questioning, but go at once? Truly we may pray:

> Within our heart of hearts
> In nearest nearness be.
> Set up thy throne within thine own;
> Go Lord; we follow thee.

VI.

The Rush of Life.

And he said unto them, Come ye yourselves apart into a desert place, and rest a while: for there were many coming and going, and they had no leisure so much as to eat.— MARK vi., 31.

It was no doubt a busy time with the apostles. They had just returned from one of their preaching journeys. They were worn out with hard work, troubled by many cares and anxieties, kept in perpetual unrest by the continual demands on their services, exhausted both in body and mind; and yet there were so many going and coming and there was so much work on hand, that they had no leisure left even to eat their meals. But their jaded and weary looks did not escape the Master's eye. Jesus, knowing their frame and remembering that they were but dust, looked compassionately on his tired followers, and bade them, "Come apart into a desert place, and rest a while;" for who knew better than he what strength can be gained amid the silent hills? And so they departed into a desert place.

A simple fact, but one which suggests an important thought. I doubt if there is anything from which this nation is suffering more to-day than from want of leisure. The apostles were busy men, but I very much question whether they went through life at such high pressure as the average Englishman does to-day. Over-excitement, over-exertion, over-straining, are doing more harm than appears on the surface, and no greater boon could be wished for this people than that they should all go apart into a desert place and rest a while.

Have you ever realized the immense change which has taken place during the last fifty or hundred years, in the rate at which men live? The change is quite as great as that from a quiet village hamlet to a noisy, bustling town. We get some indication of it if we compare the letters which people used to write fifty years ago with the hurried notes they write to-day. A letter of the old sort was no small matter. It contained a full chronicle of the writer's doings, descriptions of the persons he had seen, or the places he had visited, criticisms on the books he had been reading, and long dissertations on various matters of mutual interest. But who has time to write such letters now-a-days? Very few of us. The art of letter-writing is passing away. Correspondence now consists for the most part of a few hurried lines on some subject of immediate importance, with all words left out which will not actually destroy the sense, and every abbreviation used which will be at all comprehensible. Or think of the difference between the kind of reading which is customary with us, and that which was customary with our grandfathers. They were not always being reminded of the shortness of life, as we are. They had long, quiet evenings when they could take life leisurely, and even indulge in the luxury of reading aloud. They perhaps did not read very much, but they read good, solid books, and read them more than once. They digested what they read, thought about it and discussed it, and thoroughly mastered it. And so I am not at all sure but that the quality of their reading was really more valuable than the quantity of ours. The immense increase which has taken place in our yearly publications is not an unmixed good. There is so much that one hardly knows what to read first. We skim books instead of honestly reading them. Or we are so occupied with the countless magazines and periodicals that we have no time left to give to the elder classics of our land. Society craves excitement. It is always demanding a new number of something. There is no rest or repose. One subject of thought succeeds another as wave follows wave.

Dr. Arnold once preached a sermon to the boys at Rugby against taking in the monthly numbers of *Nicholas Nickleby*. He did it by way of protest against uninterrupted excitement. The excessive thirst for new and dazzling writing is not a healthy one, and we must regret to see how the old folio is entirely superseded by the modern pamphlet. We read too carelessly and too much. If we read less and thought more we should be really wiser men and women. Moreover, one cannot see with satisfaction that our wisest thinkers are spending their strength over fragmentary and ephemeral essays in magazines, instead of producing any thorough and lasting work. The incomplete and temporary character of their writings will prevent these from ever taking a place beside the literature of past generations.

We boast much of the improvements of modern civilization, but we must remember that besides their undoubted advantages they have also their drawbacks. Consider what a complete revolution in life has been made by the increased facilities of locomotion which we now enjoy. It is only about a hundred and twenty years since the first stage-coach ran between Liverpool and London; running once a week, and taking four days to accomplish the journey. The same journey now is traversed several times in the course of a single day, and is performed in less than five hours. The advantages of this rapid travelling are obvious, and it is easy to dilate on the blessings of steam and speed: but we seldom take into account the waste and havoc which they make in "plain living"—how they practically shorten the days of a man.

Look, again, at the universal competition of the present day. St. Paul likened life to a race, but the pace has been increased since his day. The world is becoming more and more like a vast competitive examination room. From the day on which a boy first goes to school to the day of his death he lives in competition with his fellows. School life is becoming more and more a round of examinations; in every trade and profession the rivalry becomes keener day by day. There is hardly a department of life into which competition does not enter.

Now I know that this has not been unproductive of good. Shams are weeded out, and idleness gets no chance. But still one cannot be quite satisfied with an ideal of life which represents the normal state of human beings to be that of struggling to get on. One cannot believe that the trampling, crushing, elbowing and treading on one another's heels which form the existing type of social life, constitute altogether the most desirable lot for man. One cannot help noticing the worried look which settles on men's faces. Even schoolboys sometimes seem jaded. Every now and then one hears of some promising young lad coming out of the contest with constitution shattered and mind enfeebled, and nearly every lunatic asylum counts among its inmates not a few men and women in whom the cord of reason has snapped asunder, owing to the tension of life becoming too great. No, undoubted as are many of the blessings of nineteenth century life, there can be no question that the high pressure at which we live is fraught with danger. We live our lives out too fast. There is too much seeking for effect. We must have results produced at once, something to show. Instead of thorough, quiet work, for the work's sake, we work only for results. We study only what will pay. We read only what will tell. We like to show all our mental goods upon the counter. And so I cannot help echoing Wordsworth's lament that "plain living and high thinking are no more," and feeling that one of the wants of the age is "the vision of a calmer, simpler beauty to tranquillize us in the midst of artificial tastes, and the draught of a purer spring to cool the flame of our excited life."

Now, mark you, I am not wishing for idleness. I hold the idler in the utmost contempt. I am speaking of leisure, and between idleness and leisure their is an important distinction. Leisure is the intermission of labour,—the breathing moment in the life of a busy man; and all that I regret is that these breathing moments are becoming so few. We are for ever driving on, and the machinery, mental and physical, will not stand it. It is a great mistake to think that leisure hours are wasted hours. They are nothing of the kind. It is then that you lay in a stock of strength. It is then that your mind yields some of its best products. Calm thinking, impartial views and healthy feelings do not originate in a hurry or a fever. For a healthy mental life, you must have times of quiet.

But if such times are necessary for our physical and mental health, still more are they essential to our religious welfare. No religious soul can do without them. Even Jesus, close as was the communion in which he lived with the Father, still felt the need of special seasons of prayer, and so went, as his custom was, into the synagogue on the Sabbath day, for the hour of quiet worship. And when his life grew especially difficult, and he felt the need of special strength, then he went up into a mountain to pray, where he might be alone with God : or amid the shades and silence of Gethsemane he wrestled with his shrinking will, and found strength to say, "Thy will be done," and to drink the bitter cup. Remember, too, how Paul in his hour of spiritual conflict, when the truth of Christianity first dawned upon him with a great awakening light, conferred not with flesh and blood, but betook himself to some solitude of Arabia. In that retirement the seed was sown of all his fruitful life. And so it has been with every great and saintly soul. All the heroes and heroines of Christianity have gained the intensity of their faith and have put on the beauty of holiness by constant communion with the Father which is in secret. In many a moment snatched from life's labours or companionships, the loving soul steals away to its heavenly Father, and holds sweet converse with him.

Now I feel sure that the hurry and rush of modern life bring with them no greater danger than that these seasons of quiet meditation and communion with God should get crowded out. The claims upon our time made by business and pleasure and the various interests of society, are so large that hundreds and hundreds of people find that they have no time left for prayer and meditation. It is not that they wilfully neglect these things, but almost unconsciously they allow their days to be quite filled up with other occupations. Life is a whirl of business and excitement, and there is no season left for communion with the Unseen. Yet surely this tyranny of the outward over the inward life, this subordination of our highest nature to the demands of business or society, is a misfortune greatly to be lamented. Surely, if we believe in a living God, in a divine presence ever about us, in an eternal life transcending the shows of this world, in spiritual realities lying too deep for the eye of sense, in a great heavenly Father whose ear is ever open to his children's cry : then it is little short of madness to live as if God were asleep, and heaven a dream, and prayer a sounding breath and nothing more. Depend upon it, there can be no such strong religious faith apart from prayer and communion with the Most High. Faith has its roots in prayer. And if you suffer the things which are seen and temporal to swallow up all converse with the things which are unseen and eternal, the tender plant of faith, choked by the cares of this world, will wither and fade, and your religion will be only a sickly, unreal thing.

And so, brethren, I would earnestly plead with you that you snatch from your busy lives times for meditation and for prayer. And I do so all the more urgently because I know how great are the temptations to neglect these things. Never believe that the time you spend in the congregation of worshippers, when your hearts go up to God in common prayer, or in the silence of your chamber, when you pass from shows and shadows into communion with the Everlasting One,—never believe that this is wasted time. Such moments are the best spent of any of your lives. They bring refreshment when you are weary, power when you are faint, comfort when you are sorrowful, hope when you are downcast, and they give you a secret strength, which keeps you calm and steadfast amid all the turmoil of life. All such seasons, when you can cross the threshold of eternal things and for a little while can be alone with God, guard with jealous care. You will find in them what Jesus found when he went up into the mountain to pray, or when his spirit conquered in Gethsemane: for God is as near to us as he was to him, and the promise is true now, as when it was uttered, that the pure in heart shall see their God.

We are told in the mystical story of the Apocalypse that there was silence in heaven for the space of half-an-hour, in allusion to which Mrs. Browning penned the beautiful prayer,

> "Vouchsafe us such a half-hour's hush alone,
> In compensation for our stormy years."

Brethren, we need such a half-hour's hush very often in these days; for the increasing press of our outward life can only be safely borne when there is an increased intensity of our life with God. Never was there such need as there is to-day for earnest and frequent contact with the deep and silent God. Never was it more necessary to seek refuge in the church and the chamber from the crowd and the noise which drown the still small voice within us, and the glare of this world which dims the lights of heaven. In silence then let us often commune with our own hearts, and be still. Let us come from the strife and the tumult and shut the door, that we may pray to our Father which is in secret. Each day a moment or two of solemn speech with God, a moment or two of silence while we stand alone with Him; just, as it were, a grasp of the Father's hand, one clear look into His loving eyes,—this it is which will consecrate our lives. In such solmen moments our truest life is lived; and out of them come strength mightier than words can tell, and peace which the world can never give, for all our toil and weariness and pain.

VII.

Francis of Assisi.

Seek ye first the kingdom of God, and his righteousness: and all these things shall be added unto you.—MATT. vi., 33.

IN the year 1182, a child was born into the world, who was destined to play a wonderful part in the history of that time. This child was Francis of Assisi, the founder of the Order of Franciscan Friars, and now a saint of the Roman Catholic Church—a dreamy, loving enthusiast, who was the means of producing one of the most remarkable religious revivals of which history has ever had to tell. I want to say a word to you about this " most blameless and gentle of saints," as Dean Milman calls him. The Pope of Rome addressed a letter to his clergy, on the occasion of the seventh centenary of St. Francis' birth, setting forth some of the lessons which he considered that the mediæval saint can teach the world to-day: and, for my part, I think that the life of St. Francis is a very suggestive one, though to me the moral does not seem quite the same as that which Leo XIII. would draw.

Let us, therefore, take a glance at this picture of the past. Here was a young man, the son of well-to-do parents, loving gaiety and ostentation, full of extravagant tastes, wild and prodigal in manner of life, spending his days uselessly and wastefully, and with as little thought of religious responsibility as was to be found in most lives in that age of spiritual darkness. Taken prisoner in some petty feud, he was detained a year in captivity, passed through a serious illness, and in his trouble and solitude found his way into the world of deeper and diviner things. He resolved to devote himself to a Christ-like life, and whatever seems strange and extravagant in his conduct is probably due to the fact that he aimed at a literal imitation rather than a spiritual following of Jesus. He determined to carry out the very letter of the Gospels. He sold all that he had and gave it to the poor. He devoted himself to poverty, his mystic "bride." He abandoned everything which men value in this life, and, clad in the garments of a poor mendicant, gave himself up to the service of the degraded and the poor. His father deemed such conduct madness, and confined him for some time in a dark room, but to no purpose. The young man at last renounced his family, and declared that henceforth he would have but "one Father,"—Him that is in heaven. No humiliation seemed too low for him. He begged at the gates of monasteries, performed the most menial offices, and even served the lepers in the hospitals with the tenderest care. Gradually the thought of subduing the whole world to the religion of Christ beamed upon his soul, and he began to fire others with his loving enthusiasm. He and eleven disciples determined to form a brotherhood: and we read how, after the fashion of that time, they thrice opened the Gospels upon the altar for some divine guidance as to the basis of their Order, lighting on the passages "Sell that thou hast and give to the poor," "Take nothing for your journey," "If any man will come after me, let him deny himself and take up his cross daily and follow me." The society was founded on the triple vow of chastity, poverty and obedience. The brethren were to own no property, were never to touch money, were to live on charity. And the very impossibility, as it seemed, of the vows, appears to have been their strength. Numbers crowded to take them, and at the first general assembly, held a few years later, five thousand members were present. It was to be the grandest missionary effort ever organized; they were to aim at nothing less than to evangelize the world. To this end these preaching friars went north, south, east and west,—Francis betaking himself to the East, where the crusading armies were waging war against the Turks, and not content until he had preached before the Sultan himself. The after-life of St. Francis it is difficult to follow; it is so overlaid with stories of miracles and exaggerated panegyric—the work of zealous but misguided admirers. But through all this overgrowth of myth and legend there always shines the light of a very loving, if somewhat mystic piety, and a very strong and beautiful, if somewhat imaginative enthusiasm.

But the work done by his followers is matter of historical fact. They succeeded in bringing about one of the greatest religious revivals that the Christian Church has ever witnessed. Those were days when the priests and ecclesiastics were sunk deep in worldliness, ignorance, idleness and debauchery, and religion was fast losing its hold over the hearts of the people. They were days also of terrible misery and hardship and oppression amongst the poor. And when these begging preachers, clad in their coarse frock of serge, came barefooted amongst the common people of the towns and cities, took up their abode, not in any fine monastery, but in mud huts in the poorest quarters of the towns; when they went abroad fearlessly tending those who were sick with fever, plague, or the more terrible scourge of leprosy; when they went in and out amongst the hovels of the poor, hearing their confessions and entreating them to forsake their sins; when they gathered the people together around the market crosses and in the streets, and preached to them, not in an unknown tongue, but in plain speech, and with earnest homely appeals such as all could understand; we can hardly wonder at the burst of enthusiasm which, not only in our English towns, but in Italy and Gaul and Asia, welcomed the advent of these Franciscan Friars. The common people heard them gladly. The churches began to be deserted. The idle monks of the old orders were put to shame by the active, self-devoted lives of the poor preachers, and a new wave of religious enthusiasm passed over all the countries of Christendom. And though it is true that the purity of the movement did not stand the test of time, so that in fifty years the vow of poverty began to be evaded, and the friars were building fine stone monasteries, and accumulating treasures, and degenerating into meddlesome beggars, to the great scandal and hindrance of religion; yet this must not blind us to the noble and wide-spread work that was done, and the splendid self-sacrifice which was shown, so long as they were true to the spirit of their founder.

Now, Hallam, the historian, speaking of St. Francis, says that he was "a harmless enthusiast, pious and sincere, but hardly of sane mind," and there can be little doubt, I think, that if a man were to act to-day just as St. Francis did seven hundred years ago he would be deemed a lunatic and confined in a madhouse. But then I am not sure whether, if a second Jesus were to appear in this nineteenth century, he would not be in danger of sharing a similar fate. There were not wanting eighteen centuries ago in Palestine those who said he had a devil and was beside himself, and I do not suppose that people would be wanting to-day to set down a life of such complete self-sacrifice as a case of religious mania. So that it does not seem to me a very satisfactory proceeding to dismiss the life of St. Francis as that of a madman. At any rate, if you do, his noble insanity appears to me a far higher and better thing than a great deal of our very ignoble, mean and worldly sanity. No! he was an enthusiast, a fanatic, if you like; but what do you mean by that? You mean, I suppose, a man carried away by one idea, a man who sees only one side of a truth, or only one half of life, and is altogether taken up with his one-sided, partial view. Such a man Francis of Assisi was. His view of life was narrow, one-sided; his espousal of poverty and mendicancy was carried to an unnatural, sometimes to an absurd, excess; he failed to understand the lines on which alone society can exist; he was a mystic, a dreamer, carried away completely and utterly by one idea. But, then, what an idea! The intense longing to realize a Christ-like life; a deep, overmastering love of God, a burning desire to serve and save his fellow men. Shall we wonder if, with those great thoughts swelling in his heart, he forgot something of the real joys and beauties of the present world, failed to appreciate the true value of the life that now is, and, amid the outward misery and the spiritual darkness of a worldly generation, pushed his unworldliness to an unreal and fanatical excess? Surely the wonder is that such an idea does not make more enthusiasts and fanatics than it does. Why, his fanaticism, his one-sidedness, his blindness, was nothing compared with our blind, one-sided, fanaticism of to-day! Here are we, men and women with immortal souls, set down upon this earth for a few short years, and living, as it were, in two worlds —one, the world of outward things, transitory and evanescent, the other, the world of spiritual realities, eternal as the heavens, and enduring for ever. And yet—is it credible?—so fascinated are we with the mere shows of time, so absorbed in our daily pleasures, in winning for ourselves a place in society, in making money or seeking fame, so completely are we taken up with the one idea of getting on in the things of this world, that our duty towards God, our discipleship to Christ, the divine brotherhood of humanity, the preparation of our souls for all that lies beyond, everything that pertains to our spiritual and eternal life, is thrust on one side and forgotten, and we give nearly our whole strength to mere temporary aims and ambitions. Nine men out of every ten are enthusiasts and fanatics in their devotion to things that are seen and temporal, and, so, when there comes along a man like Francis of Assisi, an enthusiast and fanatic for the sake of things that are unseen and eternal, we declare, forsooth, that his enthusiasm is madness and his fanaticism folly. Good heavens! which is the madder enthusiasm, which is the more foolish fanaticism, which is the more fatal one-sidedness,—that of this gainless lover of God, or that of our modern godless lover of gain? Surely it is just the dull, practical, common sense, worldly-minded people of to-day, the people who can see in the life of Francis of Assisi only the vagaries of a pious lunatic, who most lamentably fail to take in the full meaning of life. For my part I do not look upon the life of this mediæval saint as one which it would be wise for us to-day to copy. But I do say that it would be far better to make the mistakes which he made in the fervour of his love for God and man, than to err with the thousands to-day who give themselves body and soul to the worship of Mammon. To this extent, therefore, I sympathize with Pope Leo's exhortation. We do not want the methods of St. Francis, but we do sorely need a larger measure of his spirit.

The mistake which Francis made, the thing which made his life unnatural and extravagant, it seems to me, was this: he endeavoured to make his life a literal imitation of the life of Jesus Christ. That was the real source of all his extravagancies and eccentricities; and it is a mistake not unfruitful of difficulty sometimes amongst Christians to-day. We find Jesus bidding men to take no thought for the morrow, to suffer themselves to be robbed without resistance, to submit quietly to any injury, to give to all who ask, to lend to all who would borrow, to forsake wife and children and home to join the disciples' band. And we read of Jesus' actual sayings and doings, and then we say to ourselves, " Yes, but to live precisely such a life to-day, would overturn the foundations of society, would make us ridiculous in the eye of the world, would necessitate the neglect of obvious duties, and be every way undesirable, if not impossible. We cannot altogether be followers of Christ."

Yes, we can. There is all the difference between following a man, and imitating, that is to say aping him. " To follow Jesus," says a Dutch writer, " is to take up his principles into our hearts, that we may, each in his own way, apply them in our lives; it is to resemble him and bear his image in obedience and trust, in love and devotion; it is to speak and act as we suppose that he would have done in our place and under our circumstances. To imitate Jesus would be as far as possible to assume his external style, to adopt his expressions as literally as possible, and faithfully repeat his actions without inquiring whether at the present time and on this occasion he would still have adopted the line of action or speech which approved themselves to him eighteen centuries ago in the land of the Jews. Such an imitation is simply an absurdity and an impossibility. Those who imitate him can never learn to follow him; those who follow him must, once for all, relinquish all idea of imitating him." Well, it seems to me that Francis of Assisi made the mistake of trying, in his love for Jesus, to imitate him, instead of to follow him. It is an easy mistake to fall into. How often you find the young man to-day, who has studied under some great teacher, content himself with aping his master's style, instead of trying to grasp his principles and to let them bear natural fruit in his own life. And what a blunder it is—what a failure it always turns out to be! So it seems to me that no man ought to try to live Jesus' life, but rather to live his own life in Jesus' spirit. And so, coming back to St. Francis, it seems to me that when the Catholic Church urges men to-day to renounce home and property and wealth, and to enter some brotherhood pledged to poverty, she only succeeds in producing poor outward imitations of the great mediæval saint. The true follower of St. Francis is rather the man, who, while labouring in some trade or profession, earning his daily bread, laying up for the time of old age, and making due provision for his children, is yet animated by an ample spirit of charity and self-sacrifice, and is always ready to give of his abundance to those who need. A St. Francis to-day would not do the same things as did the St. Francis of seven hundred years ago. And a Jesus of London or Liverpool would live a different life from that of Jesus of Galilee. Only the spirit would be the same. And in all discipleships we must take care lest in copying the outward form, which is unessential, we miss the inner spirit, which is the really vital thing.

And there is one other mistake which, I think, St. Francis fell into. At the time of his illness and conversion I suppose he realized that there was a strong opposition between living for worldly and living for spiritual good,— the result being the total change in his manner of life. But I don't think he quite understood the real nature of that opposition. He imagined, I take it, as the great majority of Christians still imagine, that the kingdom of this world and the Kingdom of God stood quite apart from one another, that there are two distinct spheres—the secular and the sacred,—and that what the man of the world does, the religious man must avoid doing. The ordinary occupations of life, the work of the office or the shop, money-making, recreation, amusement,—these belong to the secular sphere, and are temptations to evil rather than opportunities for good; whereas preaching, praying, works of charity, deeds of conventional benevolence, reading devout books, attending public worship, are sacred acts, constituting the main occupations of the religious life. And the two spheres, in the orthodox conception, stand quite apart from one another, so that a man is constantly having to choose between them, and in order to get into the one must quit the other. St. Francis, in order to enter into the kingdom of heaven, thought it necessary to renounce all the common obligations and customs of the world. The Catholic monk or nun of to-day deems it needful to forsake the ordinary duties of life, in order to live a life of religion. The so-called evangelical goes about his business and his pleasure, it is true, but it is with an uneasy conscience, as though he had got into a world with which God and religion had nothing to do, and from which the sooner he runs away the better. All fall into the same error. The Kingdom of God does not stand apart from our common life. It is a spirit and a principle pervading and regulating our life. It is not quenching our natural appetites, stamping out our affections, renouncing the ordinary methods of our life, giving up natural aims and occupations and pursuits. It is simply the maintenance among them all of a divine order and proportion and harmony, so that we may do every duty faithfully, seek every object of our desire worthily, and live all our life "as ever in our great Task-Master's eye." Religion is not a new sphere of life. There is only one life; and religion is the highest law and the truest spirit, by which and in which that life can be lived. To become a saint, therefore, there is no need to change the outward sphere, only the inward spirit of your life.

And so, I do not think that Pope Leo did very wisely to point to St. Francis of Assisi as an outward pattern of life. His outward life was an extravagance even in his day, and would be an absurdity in ours. But his spirit,—his superb self-devotion, his intense enthusiasm, his mighty trust in God—that was magnificent, sublime, a thing to strive after in all ages. And that was the real secret of his power. He was grandly in earnest. No self-sacrifice could daunt him. He poured out his life in his work. And so men believed him and trusted him, and the flame of his enthusiasm spread from soul to soul, and wrought a great redeeming work. That is the secret of all revivals. It was so with the Wesleys. It was so, in its beginning, with the Salvation Army. And it must be so with us, it must be so with the Christian Church at large, before we can hope to do any great work for the Kingdom of God. When the members of our various churches in this land believe in their religion earnestly enough to sacrifice wealth and position and life in its behalf, then they will be able to move the hearts of all those to whom God is now only a name, and to lead thousands, where now they lead tens, into His Kingdom of righteousness and peace.

VIII.

Sunshine.

Truly the light is sweet, and a pleasant thing it is for the eyes to behold the sun.—ECCLES. xi.,.7.

EVEN the writer of Ecclesiastes, the great pessimist preacher of Israel, has to bear testimony to the glory of the sunshine, and though he urges his hearers to bethink them of the dark days to come, he is bound to confess that the light is a sweet and glorious thing while it lasts. Paint the world as black as he can, he feels that it is a truly pleasant thing for the eyes to behold the sun. And, indeed, the daily miracle of sunlight is very beautiful and very wonderful—even when it comes to us through a canopy of cloud and mist, with its splendour darkened and subdued and its golden glory turned into a quiet and sober gray. But far more beautiful and far more wonderful is the miracle, not of sunlight merely but of sunshine,—the grand full-orbed splendour of the great monarch of the sky as he showers his golden rays unhindered upon the laughing and rejoicing earth. Why, if sunshine, instead of being so common a gift, were a thing to be witnessed only once perhaps in a lifetime, what preparations we should make for beholding the wondrous sight! How we should leave our books, our business and our pleasure, and turn out in thousands to gaze on the unwonted spectacle and admire its strange transfiguring effects! And when the memorable occasion was past, how we should talk it over amongst ourselves, tell one another of its magnificence with fervent heart and eloquent tongue, and record the special feature of the scene that impressed our minds the most! One of us would remember how we saw the fiery orb first break from behind the morning hills, touching each peak with purple light, and making every rock and crag a pinnacle of glory. Another would tell how he watched it as it settled down into the western sea, while it traced a path of shining beauty over the dancing, sparkling waves, and touched the evening sky with flaming tints of crimson and of gold. And others would remember how even in the busy town and dusty streets, it flooded the dingy roofs and walls with transfiguring light and bathed in radiance the commonest thing on which the blessing of its smile could fall. Such an event would be an age-long wonder; and religious souls would lift their thankful song to God for this new token of his love, and praise Him with joyful heart for so wonderfully manifesting himself as a God of Light and Beauty.

But the miracle, instead of happening once in a lifetime, is one of the commonest things of our life, and so, like all common blessings, is very rarely valued at its worth. We will go miles to see a fine painting, but we scarcely deign to notice the sunlit scenes of beauty that adorn the actual world in which we live. Fine pictures are comparatively rare, but sunshine is so common that we seldom stop to think how wonderful and beautiful it is. And yet it does sometimes happen, I think, that in the early springtide, when the dull, gloomy winter seems suddenly to come to an end, and we emerge all at once into a spell of bright and sunny days, the quick, sharp contrast arrests our attention, and we in some measure realise what a glorious gift the sunshine is. Some thought of this kind is apt to pass through our minds in the first fresh and sunny days of early spring. We all seem to be really rejoicing in the cloudless skies and welcome beams, and to be able to realise what an enormous difference sunshine makes in the world. One day we look abroad and the sky is veiled by sullen clouds, the cold wind is driving over the plain, and storms of pelting rain are beating on the bare wet trees and sodden grass. Nature looks as if she were mourning and weeping and hiding her face in pain. The whole scene is desolate and melancholy, and its gloom seems to reach and infect our own hearts, and cast a darkness on our daily path. But the next day, what a change! You look upon the same landscape. But is it really the same? There are the same features, the same fields, the same hills, the same river, the same trees and houses and streets. But how transfigured! No longer gray and dismal, they are now all bright and glorious. The earth seems fairly laughing with delight, and the fields break forth into gladness and singing. The trees put out their bright green buds, the flowers open their bosoms to the light, the leaden sky is changed to soft transparent blue, and our human hearts open their windows to the universal gladness that is all about us, and join in nature's praise. What has wrought this wondrous transformation? Simply the sunshine —merely sunshine. Sunshine has converted a desert into a paradise. The gloom has gone, the storms have passed away, the frown has vanished from nature's face, the birds renew their song, and all is bright and gay. because the light of heaven is on the earth.

Well, now, it seems to me that if you have felt anything of this, if your heart has anyway been touched by the charm of the fresh spring sunshine, if you have at all realised its transfiguring power, you will easily be able to enter into the analogous but far deeper thought to which this other should lead us,—the thought of the charm and grace of spiritual sunlight, the sunshine of the heart; and you will see that just as the natural sunshine irradiates the face of nature, so spiritual sunshine transfigures and glorifies our life. Ask yourself whether this be not so. Is it not a pleasant thing to dwell in moral and spiritual sunshine? Do we not love to be with sunny people—people whose hearts are warm and bright and open, people with kind, cheerful voices and glad faces and hopeful, uncomplaining souls? Do not our hearts open to receive the joyous influence that goes out from natures such as these, and does it not soften us into love and kindness, brighten us into cheerfulness, and drive away all harsh words and tones of lamentation, as the sun chases the mist up the mountain side, until a glad and joyful feeling reigns triumphant in our souls? Yes, if natural sunshine is a boon, spiritual sunshine is one far more. For it gladdens and irradiates the inner man. Of course I know that we must have clouds and storms as well, and that these have their uses and bring their blessings. God sends us tears as well as laughter, and the showers of sorrow and the wintry days of trial come fraught with blessings as surely as the joys of summertide; and our souls need the darkness of the night as well as the brightness of the noonday. But, none the less, sunshine is a good and pleasant thing, and it would be well if we would let the clouds and the darkness be all of God's sending, and not make them artificially for ourselves. And, believe me, this power to make sunshine or gloom is really ours. Go into twenty homes one after another, and in how many of them will the shadows be God-given, in how many will you find a mere man-made darkness? It is not the great trials and sharp griefs coming down to us from heaven that envelop us with any lasting gloom. Hundreds of men have borne these and are yet cheerful people with plenty of sunshine in their hearts. The shadows that God sends are comparatively few. In nine cases out of ten we make our own gloom—for ourselves and for one another, and we ourselves shut out the sunlight that God meant to be in our hearts. The obscuring clouds are simply the evil exhalations of our own peevishness and sin. The lack of sunlight in our homes is not of God's doing. It comes from our own fretfulness and bad temper and evil thoughts and cold hard unlovely ways. And it is these things that really, in the great majority of cases, make our homes dull and dismal. Look at the cold, discontented, ill-tempered man. See how he darkens God's spiritual sunshine. When you go into his presence it is like passing into a fog. All the sweetness of life seems absent, and a cold, dark chill settles on your soul. And then look at the man of cheerful temper and kindly heart, ever a smile in his eye and a pleasant word upon his lip and a loving purpose in his soul. What a charm there is in his companionship! Light, life, warmth are all about him, and our hearts rejoice to warm themselves in the cheery glow. Oh friends, it is a perfectly God-like faculty, this of making sunshine. There is hardly anything, it seems to me, that one could wish for oneself better than this, to be remembered by one's friends as one who always left a streak of sunshine behind him wheresoever he was and wheresoever he went. So remembered one might die content. And this is a matter, to a large extent, in our own power. We can accustom ourselves to look at things on the best and brightest side, to think the best, and not the worst, of people's motives and desires, to make the best of our own lot and our own troubles, and as we run the race of life to " put a cheerful courage on." All this will help us, and we can remember that our God is a God of joy and light and beauty, and that in no way can we serve Him better than by making the world a gladder, brighter, sunnier place.

But if we want to illumine the dark places of earth, and make other men's lives brighter, then we must have plenty of sunshine in our own souls; and sunshine, too, of a particular sort—bright, unfading, independent of all changes, clear of all shadows, shining through all storms, even the true light from heaven, the sunshine of God's presence in our hearts. And I cannot help thinking that one reason why there is so little spiritual sunshine and so much spiritual gloom in the world of men, is just this: that God's presence is not felt as a sunshine at all, that the thought of Him has not been regarded as a thing to fill the soul with gladness, that religion has been made a matter of gloom and terror, rather than of gladness, light and love.

Bethink you what the character of the popular religion has been—a thing to be dismal about, to speak of with sighs and tears and saddened tones, a theme terrible, and fit to make one miserable; to be contemplated periodically for the soul's health, but to be escaped from as soon as possible in order to get back to brighter and pleasanter topics. That is not the kind of religion we want. We need a simple, hearty faith in God that is so free from terror and so full of gladness that to turn to it is always a source of joy and thankfulness. And religion, rightly understood, is this—a glorious and joyful thing, not a restraint but an outlet for our love, not a saddening cloud but a gladdening and ever-brightening light. I do not believe that I am judging unfairly—I certainly try not to do so—but the more I think of it the more disastrous seems to me the mischief which orthodoxy has done in this respect. It has put forth representations of God and his dealings with men which have made religion the saddest and most melancholy thing conceivable, instead of being an inspiration of hope and joy; and no man who really believes in the orthodox dogmas can have one gleam of sunshine in his soul. Once to realise them would be to go mad with horror and despair. Do you think that is too strong a statement? Let us turn for a moment to a characteristic sermon preached by Mr. Spurgeon. Mr. Spurgeon is an outspoken, honest man and never flinches from the consequences of his creed. He believes that faith in the atoning sacrifice of Christ is the sole condition of salvation, and that all who lack that faith are lost eternally. The saved must be believers in Jesus, and he defines believers as those who believe "that God must punish sin, that God has punished sin in the person of Jesus, and that he has therefore set forth his son Jesus Christ to be a propitiation for sin, that whosoever believeth in him might not perish but have everlasting life." This, he says, is the main point in the character of those who have everlasting life. They are not said to do anything or achieve anything, but they believe in Jesus the Christ. And further on he continues: "Did I hear some one object, 'You make too much of so small a matter as believing. You make out that simply by trusting in Jesus Christ there is a difference made between one man and another of a most extraordinary kind, and that it is made at once'? Yes, I do say that, exactly that, and, so far as I am concerned, I do not care how much you quarrel with it, I shall not tone down the statement: 'He that believeth and is baptized shall be saved : but he that believeth not shall be damned.'"

Could you ask for any clearer or any sadder faith? This great preacher believes that every year hundreds and thousands of God's children, including perhaps dear friends of his own, are going down into eternal perdition, because they do not believe in this theological dogma of the atonement: and he believes that God is fiend enough to carry out this decree! Why such a faith, if I believed it, would break my heart! Talk of religion as a source of gladness! Such a religion would wrap my whole life in a shroud of gloom. How any man who believes such doctrines—believes that human souls all about him are swinging on the verge of an eternal precipice, can give any attention to the price of shares and the vicissitudes of cotton, or ever suffer a smile to pass across his face, it passes my comprehension to know. I suppose very few orthodox people do thoroughly realise the consequences of their creeds. Only so can their conduct be explained.

But are not such terrible doctrines calculated to take the sunshine out of life? And would the thought of Mr. Spurgeon's God put anything but gloom and sadness in your soul? Surely we ought to rejoice in our happier faith—faith in a God of infinite love and mercy, who will not suffer even the greatest sinner to be an exile for ever, much less one who has simply erred in his belief—a God not to be thought of with dread, as a wrathful Avenger; but with love as a tender Father—a God the remembrance of whom can bring no shade of sadness, but only a blessed trust in His unutterable love. May God grant that there may grow up in our hearts such a perfect reliance on His goodness, and such a true and earnest faith in His Fatherly care, that all our lives may be lived in that Divine Presence, which to those who really feel it, is one unbroken sunshine of hope and gladness and peace!

IX.

Is Life worth Living?

Having promise of the life that now is, and of that which is to come.—I. TIMOTHY iv., 8.

THE life that now is, this spell of years, few or many, which you and I are to spend upon this earth,—how are we to regard it? As a blessing or as a curse? As a precious boon for which to thank God daily, or as a weary drudgery from which to beg Him to "remove us early to our place of rest"? As a barren wilderness to be passed over as soon as possible, or as a place fertile with the fruits of goodness and blessing? In other words, Is this life worth living—a thing to be glad of and thankful for? or is it not worth living—a thing to be despised and escaped from as soon as possible?

You may wonder that anyone should ask so strange a question; but it is a question which humanity has not always answered in the same way. Away in the East there are thousands, aye millions, of people to-day, the fundamental article of whose religious creed is that life is a curse; that the world is very evil and not worth living in. The Buddhists, who far out-number the entire body of Christendom, believe, and teach it as a fundamental principle of their faith, that the greatest blessing which a man can win is a state of practical non-existence. To escape the weary burden of life, the dreary round of years and months and days, and to enter the eternal sleep of Nirvana, is their highest conception of joy, and the end of all their religious hopes and prayers. But we need not go to India or China to find men and women who hold that life is not worth living. There are no doubt thousands here in England to-day who, crushed down by life's burdens, or sick at heart with the weary struggle for existence, and with no strong inward faith to buoy them up, have come to look upon life as a worthless gift; men and women who are so tired of the strife and sorrow and sin that they would lie down to-night with a grand sense of relief could they believe that no morning sun would ever waken them again to take up the burden which has crushed their hearts so long. And of such I would speak very tenderly. The world does sometimes seem to deal very hardly with her children; and I cannot wonder if, walking on such dark and troubled waters, their faith should falter and their souls should sink. They are wrong in their conclusion, but their error is not altogether without excuse.

But there is another class of persons who take this view with whom I have not so much sympathy. I mean literary men who argue in cold blood that life is not worth living, in sumptuous drawing rooms or in the pages of the quarterly reviews, and empty worldlings who live for nothing but to find a new sensation, who wake up in the morning asking how they shall kill time for another day, and have no aim or end or object in life but their own selfish pleasure. I do not wonder that such men come to doubt the value of life, for certainly life as they live it is not worth living in the least. They squander it in vanity and selfishness. Who can be surprised that the result should be vexation of spirit?

And then, besides, we have churches and theologies trying to persuade men even against their own experience that life is not worth living. One of the favourite devices of orthodoxy is to quicken the desire for the heavenly life by pouring contempt upon this life on earth. This life is represented as a weary desert, a valley and shadow of death, a mournful banishment, a realm of darkness and danger.

> Prickly thorns through all the ground
> And mortal poisons grow;
> And all the rivers that are found
> With dangerous waters flow.

Religious phraseology is full of the survivals of this mode of thought and feeling, and orthodox hymnology is pervaded by it almost from end to end. This life is the type of all that is mean and low and base. How many otherwise admirable hymns are almost spoiled for present use by phrases which express an altogether unnatural and irreligious depreciation of this world? The natural affections of humanity, intellectual ability, the desire for comfort, beauty, wealth, art, pleasure, are all comprised in the designation " this world," and visited with a common condemnation. The whole energy and enthusiasm of religion have been engrossed by thoughts of heaven, and only the merest dregs reserved for earthly things. This world is hollow and worthless : have as little to do with it as possible ; concentrate your affections on the world to come—that has been the teaching most common in the Christian Church. And not only is this the tone of a past theology ; it is still the teaching, in more or less modified or unmodified form, to be heard in many branches of the Christian Church. If you want to hear it in all its nakedness, go to Mr. Mallock, whose book became so famous some time ago. He tells us plainly that life in itself is a disaster and a curse, and that the only thing that can make it worth having at any price is a belief in the Roman Catholic Church. Or go to Mr. Moody, the revivalist, and he will tell you bluntly that this life is not worth having at all, and that the world is a miserable failure and fiasco, unless you accept his eternity as a supplement to the life you are living here.

Now, friends, I hold that this way of thinking is not only a blunder but an impiety. There are a few poor, weary, worn strugglers on whom the conditions of life have pressed with peculiar severity, who, as I have said, must not be judged hardly if they fall into this mistake. But that men should pervert life from its true purposes, waste it in frivolity and self-seeking, and then come and tell us that God's gift is not worth having, and that life is vanity ; and that Christian Churches should give encouragement to so irreligious a thought is a thing altogether intolerable. To the great masses of men the life that now is, unless it be grossly abused, is a most precious boon, and it is only a morbid character or a morbid theology which can make it appear a curse. To look at the matter in the roughest way, the almost universal desire for life makes the question whether life is worth living an absurdity. When Horace Greeley was once asked how he judged whether he had succeeded or not in any particular lecture he replied, "I think I have succeeded when more people stay in than go out." A similar test might roughly be applied to life. The vast majority of men desire life, desire to stay in rather than to go out. Life is therefore a blessing and not a curse, and Tennyson's words are true :

> 'Tis life whereof our nerves are scant;
> O life, not death, for which we pant;
> More life, and fuller, that we want.

Let us look at this a little more closely. I do not believe that there is any healthy man, woman, or child who, apart from his or her theology, would not be ready to declare that life is worth living for its own sake ; that, quite apart from any hope of future reward, it is a grand, blessed thing to live. Have you ever stood on some hill-top and seen river and valley and broad expanse of ocean stretched out at your feet in summer glory? Have you ever gazed into the midnight sky, resplendent with the moon walking in her brightness or " thick inlaid with patins of bright gold "? Have you ever walked through the woods on a bright spring morning and rejoiced with the singing of the birds? Have you stood by the sea and felt the breezes on your brow, and watched the breakers tumbling in upon the shore? Have you looked into the laughing eyes of little children and heard their shouts of joy and seen the delight they experience simply in breathing and living? Have you felt the grasp of a companion's hand and experienced the joys of sympathy and friendship? Have you gathered with dear ones round the Christmas fire, and understood the wealth of love and meaning conveyed in that one word " Home ? " Have you felt the exalted joy which comes of every deed or thought of self-sacrifice and kindness? Have you, in short, ever tasted what it means to live, and have you not been able to say, " Yes! this is unspeakably good. No matter what I am, no matter whither I go, this life that now is is a thing to thank God for from the bottom of my heart." I believe that would be the natural feeling of every healthy mind. I know that life has also its sadnesses. But these are fleeting as the clouds; the joys are always present like the background of eternal sky. The misfortunes and calamities of life are told and chronicled as "news"; the happiness we take as a matter of course and say nothing about it, it is so common. I know, too, that there are terrible bereavements, but it is "better to have loved and lost than never to have loved at all," and even the bitterness of bereavement is a testimony to the joy which has gone before it. Take it all round, life is a boon and blessing, worth living, worth improving, worth employing, worth consecrating with high endeavour and earnest work. That is the natural verdict of the faithful heart. And I would ask is not this the true verdict? And has theology any right to step in and issue her black libels on this fair gift of God? For, friends, those preachers who glorify heaven by vilifying earth, who make this life nothing in order to make the next life everything, are issuing a libel. The life that now is is not merely a breath, a tale that is told, a barren wilderness, or a bubble burst; it is a blessing, just as surely as is the life to come. It is the most certain thing that I know of in this universe; it is a drama whose consequences run out into eternity. A man who lives truly must always rejoice to live. It seems to me that a theory which makes out that this life is a curse is exceedingly little removed from an atheistic theory. We can only judge of the next world from what we know of this. And if you can see only evil at the heart of all things here, if the world is bad, and humanity bad, and the outcome of all things bad, then I do not see what ground you have for supposing that heaven will be any better. If you cannot believe in the goodness of God in this world, which is all you know, why should you believe in it at all? You might as well say that you admire the genius of Handel, but you don't care for the *Messiah* or for any other composition of his which you have ever heard. All you know of God is from what He has done for you in this world, and if that is not worth having, or worse, then I cannot see why you should believe in the goodness of God at all. For myself, if I could not believe in God here and now, believe that His loving-kindness has set me where I am, and encompasses my path with good to-day, if I could not believe in the blessing of the present hour, then neither could I believe in God at all.

It is just because I have experienced God's goodness here that I can perfectly trust that goodness for all the great hereafter.

And believe it, friends, whatever the theologies may teach, it is not the truest seers who have said hard things about this world. It is men like Byron, or the writer of Ecclesiastes, or perhaps even puzzled Job sitting in his ashes; but you hear no such teaching from Jesus Christ, the clearest-eyed prophet that ever looked into this world's heart. The most striking fact about Jesus' teachings is that they were almost all for helping and improving this world and that he hardly ever spoke of the future at all. Clearly he wanted men to believe in a present Kingdom of God.

And so, friends, my answer to the question, "Is life worth living?" is, Yes! I am in the world and I am glad of it, and the more I see of it the more I believe in it, and the more I thank God for his precious gift. And if, brethren, life ever seems to you dry and barren, hollow and worthless, and you think to yourself, "O that I had wings like a dove, for then would I fly away and be at rest"; let me say that I don't think getting away would mend the matter at all, for the mischief is probably in yourself. You have probably never set yourself seriously to get at the heart of this life's meaning, or to find out all the depth of goodness and blessing which it contains. Instead of running away from it, try to get into the heart of it. Enter joyfully into its duties; sympathise with its sorrows; help on its holy victories; look, not for its shadows only, but for its light: so shall you come at last to thank your Heavenly Father for His gift of life, and to own that it is very good.

One word more. We are told by these same very orthodox folk, who are so fond of depreciating this world, that the only thing that solaces them in this barren wilderness is the thought of the eternity beyond. And yet, do you know, if there is one thing which would make me feel that life was not worth living, it would be to believe in the orthodox heaven and hell. Good as life seems to me in itself, grand and glorious as it seems to me when supplemented by the thought of future progress to perfection in a life to come, I would rather never have been born at all than think of life

as supplemented in the way the old hell-dogma would have
us believe. That thought would make life a curse. I would
rather sleep in death for ever than wake to find the songs of
the redeemed eternally mocked by the cries of tormented
souls in hell. And so I am convinced would every true-
hearted man. Take the thought expressed in a little poem
called the Self-exiled, and say if it be not a Christ-like one.

> "Now open the gate and let her in,
>   And fling it wide,
> For she hath been cleansed from stain of sin,"
>   St. Peter cried.
>   And the angels all were silent.
>
> "Though I am cleansed from stain of sin,"
>   She answered low,
> "I came not hither to enter in,
>   Nor may I go."
>   And the angels all were silent.
>
> * * * * *
>
> "But I may not enter there," she said;
>   "For I must go
> Across the gulf where the guilty dead
>   Lie in their woe."
>   And the angels all were silent.
>
> "If I enter heaven I may not speak
>   My soul's desire
> For them that are lying, distraught and weak,
>   In flaming fire."
>   And the angels all were silent.
>
> "Should I be nearer Christ," she said,
>   "By pitying less
> The sinful living or woful dead
>   In their helplessness"?
>   And the angels all were silent.
>
> "Should I be liker Christ, were I
>   To love no more
> The loved, who, in their anguish, lie
>   Outside the door?"
>   And the angels all were silent.
>
> "Should I be liker, nearer Him,
>   Forgetting this,—
> Singing all day with the seraphim
>   In selfish bliss?"
>   And the angels all were silent.

Yes, friends, eternity under such conditions is a thing for a brave man to fling away. If he might not help to wipe away the tears and stay the pains of the lost, at least he would wish to sleep for ever that he might not know of their anguish or hear their cries. Thank God that we have been delivered from such a nightmare as this. For us the life that now is is no barren waste to be escaped from as soon as possible, but a land fruitful in all good things and worthy of all diligent cultivation ; and as for the life that is to come, though no man has pierced its mysterious veil, we, at least, believe that it will be ordered by the same Power of love and mercy which has always encircled our life on earth.

X.

Indifference.

I know thy works, that thou hast a name that thou livest, and art dead.—Rev. iii., 1.

These words were addressed to a church: but whether you are considering a church or an individual there can hardly be a worse spiritual plight to be in than that which we so often hear described as dead-alive, living in name, but to all intents and purposes dead. Never is a church in a more dangerous condition than when she retains the outward forms of piety, after having lost the inner spirit. Never is a man further from the Kingdom of God than when he carries under the cloak of his religion a careless, irreverent, unprayerful heart. For in such cases the outward veneer and polish conceal the dry-rot within, and not only deceive other people but often impose on the man himself.

This state of spiritual death, however,—or rather spiritual torpor, for the soul is never so dead but that it may be aroused to life again,—may easily be confounded with two other very different things: and care should be taken not unjustly to mistake the latter for the former. There are people, as we all know, who are constitutionally cold and unenthusiastic, who in all things alike are passive and inert. Take them when you will, in what department of life you will, you find it almost impossible to arouse them to any fervour, or to kindle in them any glow of excitement. Even the things that interest them most are unable to ruffle the lethargic calm of their character.

Such people are naturally equally cold and stolid in their religious feelings. They have no very vivid spiritual experiences. They neither climb the heights of ecstasy nor sound the depths of remorse. But they are by no means spiritually dead. They are as much alive to spiritual things as they are to anything else. If they do not respond readily to the invitations of faith, they are equally slow to yield to the seductions of sin. They fulfil the commandment. They love God with all their heart and soul and mind and strength, and, if that all does not stand for much, still it represents the whole of what they have, and that is all that is asked. To accuse them of spiritual death, because the fire of their spiritual life burns somewhat slowly, is to do them a great injustice.

Again, we must not mistake for spiritual death a certain reserve which is very common in speaking about religious subjects. The man who talks the most is not, as a rule, the man who feels the most. Rather is the opposite true. Very deep feelings are rarely heard glibly on the tongue. It is one of the most difficult things with most of us to talk freely about the inmost things of our spiritual life. We cannot find language in which to express ourselves. We do not always feel sure of a sympathetic hearing. We shrink from laying bare to the rude gaze of men the holiest secrets of our hearts, and the deepest springs of our life. We dare not expose the tenderest flowers of our faith to the rough winds of publicity or the ungentle handling of the world. Occasionally, it is true, one meets with people who seem to like talking about their religious experiences, and I suppose one ought not to question their sincerity. But, generally, I should credit with a deeper religious life the man who only hints at the feelings which he reverently hides, than him who professes to turn his soul inside out that all the world may see.

I admit that this reserve on religious topics, this shrinking from giving expression to our religious feelings, may easily be carried too far. I believe that in our own churches this is very often the case, and that we are now suffering to some extent from an over-delicacy in this respect. I often wish very much that we could talk to one another more easily and more freely than we do about our spiritual life and the deep things of God—not about theology; we can talk easily enough about that—but about religion and the inner conflicts and feelings and aspirations of our religious life. I am afraid we lose a good deal of mutual help through our reticence. Still I am satisfied that it is an error on the right side. It is a healthy, if distorted reverence that closes our lips; and I would far rather see this than the over-familiar and often irreverent handling of the most sacred things which sometimes characterizes the Methodist class-room. There is something, at any rate, to be said for the feeling, expressed in the preacher's words, "God is in heaven and thou upon earth, therefore let thy words be few."

Neither of these things, therefore, is to be confounded with spiritual death. That apostolic phrase may be translated into the modern English "religious indifference." It is a sleep or torpor which comes over the spiritual faculties, and destroys their vital functions. The man is alive to everything else, alive to claims of pleasure and ease, to the love of beauty, wealth, or power, is alive intellectually, is a good astronomer, or physician, or statesman, but that part of his nature which stands related to God and eternity is numb and inactive. His spiritual faculties are palsied. His soul is asleep. It is not a general, constitutional apathy, or a shrinking reserve. It is a deadness of his religious consciousness.

From this spiritual apathy, this religious indifference, the churches have more to fear than from anything else. An insidious disease within is far more dangerous than an open attack from without. A little opposition, a certain amount of persecution, a few difficulties to contend against, is often a very good thing for a church. Its members are put upon their mettle. They feel that they have a work to do, and a victory to win, and that each man must be at his post. They see that they are responsible for the failure or success of their organization or their principles, and that there must be no lagging behind, no self-seeking, no love of present gain or ease, no compromise with the world, no dallying with temptation, but a brave heart and a steady eye, and an unyielding perseverance, if the field is to be really won. The time when a church is despised and unpopular, and striving to make good its claims, is, as a rule, the time of its strongest and healthiest religious life. Large demands are made on the courage and self-denial of its adherents, demands which only men and women of deep convictions and really in earnest can fulfil. Those who are half-hearted, who look back after putting their hand to the plough, are not fit for such a Kingdom of God.

But in these days of religious toleration, when we sit every man under his own theological vine and fig-tree, and there are none to make us afraid, when to belong to the most heretical church involves no very large amount of martyrdom, and to be orthodox none at all ; in these days, when the Church is honoured and her claim established, when it costs a man absolutely nothing to be a Christian, when to own the name of Christ is no longer a mark of brave self-sacrifice, but rather a social advantage than otherwise : there is no little danger that the churches will be filled with hollow conformists, men, who, caring nothing whatever for religion, call themselves Christians because it is respectable, appear in their pews on Sunday, not because they hunger for communion, but because they want to do what is fashionable, who put on the outward garb of Christianity without taking its spirit into their hearts, who have a name that they live, but who, all the while, are spiritually dead. Nay, this is more than a danger. It is an existing disease. Naturally the fashionable churches suffer most. But none are free from it. In every church you may find some to whom religion is a mere outside varnish, a matter for the lips and not for the heart, who no more realize the meaning of the deep words of contrition which they sing—the sigh of the penitent spirit, the yearning for a Divine Love, the taking of the meek disciple's vow—than the pipes of the organ comprehend the sweet strains they utter ; on whose souls the living words of psalmist, prophet and apostle make as little impression as they do on the stone pillars of this church ; who are as far from grasping the great gospel of Christ and making it the motive power of their lives, as are the wooden pews in which they sit. Brethren, it is these nominal Christians who are the Church's greatest danger to-day. It is these people with only a name to live, mere dry skeletons clad in religious drapery, who are her most serious weakness. It is this sham, make-believe Christianity that is sapping her strength and undermining her walls. The churches of this nineteenth century are drooping for want of a keener and more earnest spiritual life, are waiting for a new flood of religious enthusiasm that shall unmask this simulated piety and bring home the great questions to every man's conscience, "Are you shamming or are you in earnest? What is the serious aim of your life? Is it to seek after holiness, come what may? Or is it to get as much ease and honour out of the world as you can, and give back the least possible toil and self-denial? Which do you really believe in, the divine wisdom as taught by Jesus, or the penny wisdom of this generation? Is this religion of yours the most real, the most solemn, the most supreme thing in all your life, or is it only a piece of dead conventionalism? Is it a firm rock on which you stand, which supports you through every stormy trial, or, instead of its supporting you, do you carry it? Is it only a dead stone which you hold in your hand, a useless fetish, an idle charm, which you drop at the first whisper of sin?"

Brethren, much as it pains me to see a man enchained in idle superstitions, oppressed by the burden of unhelpful dogmas and the fetters of cramping creeds: sorry, as I am, on the other hand, to find a man doubting or denying what appear to me holy and helpful truths, I would rather see him in either of these cases, I would rather have him steeped in superstition or given over to scepticism, than resigned to dwell in that spiritual lotus-land of religious indifference. There is a fatal slumber of the spirit which is worse than bigotry, and more deadly than doubt.

We Unitarians are apt to lay not a little stress on the power of truth and the importance of a rational faith. And therein I think we do wisely. But need I remind you that it must be living truth, truth that is wrought into our very lives? Mere abstract truth, truth that is wrapped up in creeds, accepted on authority, received as a tradition, will do very little for a man. It must come home to him personally, it must be a matter of inward experience, if it is to be such as he can live by. I should care very little to give men more enlightened opinion unless I believed that I thereby helped to quicken their faith. And when this does not happen, when, as a man advances to larger truths, he comes to have a weaker spiritual life, there is nothing to rejoice in, but everything to deplore. He had far better have kept his orthodoxy, if so doing he had kept his faith. It is no use your making him a wiser theologian unless in so doing you also make him a better Christian. Living error is, after all, better than dead truth. Deadness is the one thing to be dreaded. While there is life, there is hope.

And so, on the other hand, I think that we have far less to fear from open and avowed scepticism than from that unbelieving indifference which hides itself under the cloak of conformity. Active, searching, vigorous doubt will often work itself clear of its difficulties, and when its stormy days and nights are over the sceptic will find himself in smooth seas of restful faith and under the serene and open face of heaven. But there is no hope for the man who neither prays, nor believes, nor thinks, nor inquires, but is simply indifferent. The dull clouds gather, the heavy mists shut him in, the thick gloom encircles him, until he can see hardly a hand-breadth before him, and the glory of the heavens is gone. And there is no chance of the spiritual atmosphere clearing, because there is neither the breath of aspiration, nor the hurricane of doubt. Assuredly the storms of unbelief are trying, but they are infinitely preferable to the dead calm of indifference. Anything is better than that.

And so I do not think we need share largely in the alarm so commonly felt in the present day at the boldness with which doubts are now expressed and the tendency of modern unbelief to come forward into the light of day. If we are to have unbelief at all, it is far better that it should be sincere and out-spoken than hushed up in a corner out of the light. It is less dangerous sailing under its own colours than flying the flag of the churches. I would rather have it outside the churches than inside. The sincere, fervent atheism of men like the late Professor Clifford is at any rate an honest, living thing. Such men, at all events, are alive to the soul's deep wants, though they seem to us in no way able to satisfy them. But the wretched indifference, the disguised atheism that appears in the church and lurks in the pew, repeating the creed and singing the hymns, is so insidious and deadly a disease, is an insensibility so hopeless that I cannot see in it one gleam of good. And if the plain, unveiled, uncompromising scepticism of the day is going to save us from this —if nineteenth century unbelief is God's plan for clearing the dull, close, heavy atmosphere, and dispelling the gloomy clouds which a selfish worldly indifference has rolled upon the churches—then I heartily welcome it. If there is no other way of putting an end to this mere nominal Christianity, of quickening our dead-alive churches, of wakening men up out of the indifference and spiritual torpor and practical atheism, which are wasting and destroying our real religious life, save by a period of keen, painful, but living doubt, then I for one gladly hail the purifying blast.

For, brethren, we need not fear lest religion should go under. We know that God lives, that truth and right must win, that faith and love can never die. Real religion is eternal as humanity, everlasting as God. As Theodore Parker once said, " It is only men's heads that swim, not the stars that run round."

And yet for the sake of this age of ours, for the sake of our nation's true happiness, for the sake of your own peace, see to it that you shall never need so severe an arousal. "What is the misery of the multitudes in Christian countries?" wrote Dr. Channing. "Not that they disbelieve Christianity, or that they hold great errors, but that truth lies dead within them. They use the most sacred words without meaning. They hear of spiritual realities, awful enough to raise the dead, with utter unconcern." Brethren, it is terribly easy to slip into this living death. The fatal slumber steals over our spirits almost before we are aware. Religion so easily becomes a matter of routine, that few of us can afford to be careless. Are there any here so sure of their steadfastness, so confident that they can keep the shield of their faith untarnished and the sword of the Spirit bright; that I may not say to you, Be vigilant, be earnest! Watch and pray!

XI.

Comfort in Religion.

The God of all comfort.—II. CORINTHIANS i., 3.

It is not uncommon to hear a comparison instituted between orthodox religion and what I may term rational religion, with respect to the amount of comfort to be derived from each; the result of the comparison being usually supposed to be greatly in favour of orthodoxy. The heterodox views of God, immortality, providence, salvation, are represented as cold and vague and unsatisfying, whereas it is supposed that the more popular beliefs on such subjects are warm, clear and full of comfort. Whatever else may be said when a man outgrows the beliefs of the popular churches and begins to hold, what the world is pleased to call, advanced opinions on religious matters; it is generally regarded as safe to assert that he has at any rate given up all that is most comfortable to believe, and that henceforward he will have to put up with a faith which, whether more rational or not, is certainly less comforting.

It must be a very comfortable assurance, for instance, to a man whose life has not been of the highest character, to be told that if he will only believe in Jesus Christ the stain of all his sins will be wiped away in the Saviour's blood. You remember how, when the pilgrim, in Bunyan's fable, staggering under the burden of his sins, came at length to a place where there stood a cross, and a little below, in the bottom, a sepulchre, his burden loosed from off his shoulders and fell from off his back and began to tumble and so continued to do till it came to the mouth of the sepulchre, where it fell in. That is the typical representation of a thought that has been of unquestionable comfort to thousands of sinning souls: the thought that however sorely we may have transgressed the laws of life, acceptance of Jesus' death as our atonement will free us from all penalties. No matter how great the debt, Jesus has paid it all, we are told. Only believe on him, trust the redeeming power of his blood, and, though your sins be as scarlet, you may enter heaven without a stain upon your souls :—a doctrine very untrue, very immoral even, as it seems to me, but undoubtedly of great consolation to those who can believe it. Far more comfortable than the theory that every sin brings its inevitable punishment, and sooner or later will find the sinner out.

Again, very comforting to many people is the dogmatic confidence and realistic precision with which some orthodox preachers talk about heaven. In order to make it real to their hearers, they think it necessary to describe it as though they had been there to see what it is like. And I have no doubt that such realistic descriptions do afford a certain amount of comfort to such as can accept them. I speak though now only of the more modern orthodox conceptions of a future life. There was nothing very enticing in the old thought of the utterly idle and inane heaven, where the redeemed spent their time between psalm-singing and contemplating the tortures of the lost. There was certainly no comfort, but a great deal of terror, connected with John Calvin's or Jonathan Edwards' thought of immortality—an immortality of heaven for the few elect and eternal misery for the millions lost. Far better be annihilated, one would think, than saved with so small a minority ; except for those who, like the Scotch minister, do not care to be " saved in a crowd."

But the more modern orthodox conception of heaven is, to a large extent, free from the old horrors, and is no doubt a genuine source of consolation to orthodox people. The only objection to it is that it is an attempt to map out and make realistic that which God has determined we shall know absolutely nothing about. The veil between earth and heaven has never been lifted, and every attempt to paint the joys of a future state is simply pure conjecture, and of no value whatever as a matter of belief. Still such attempts are made and accepted, and become a source of comfort. Some years ago a small book, entitled *The Gates Ajar*, obtained an immense circulation, and, I believe, brought comfort to thousands of people. It contained a most intensely realistic representation of the heavenly life; one of the characters, I remember, a little girl, being assured that she should have a piano in heaven. Of course there can be no intrinsic objection to celestial pianos which would not tell equally against celestial harps, but the instance strikes one as a *reductio ad absurdum* of the practice of describing heaven in terms of earth, unless your descriptions are understood to be merely poetical and imaginative. Adelaide Proctor, most tender of Roman Catholic singers, has given us some exquisite fancies about the unknown future, but we must always remember that they are only fancies, not facts. Writing about "the children's place in heaven," she says that it is

> At Mary's feet, who softly sings
> A little chant to please them, low and sweet,
> Or, smiling, strokes their little angel wings,
> Or gives them her white lilies or her beads,
> To play with: yet, in spite of flower or song,
> They often lift a wistful look that pleads
> And asks her why their mother stays so long.
> Then our dear Queen makes answer, "She will call
> "Her very soon;" meanwhile they are beguiled
> To wait and listen while she tells them all
> A story of her Jesus as a child.

That is a beautiful, a most tender thought, and, I have no doubt, exceedingly full of consolation to a devout Roman Catholic who implicitly believes it, but of course it is absolutely without foundation as a real picture of heaven. And so of all pictures of heaven. They are attempts to paint what human eye has never seen, and afford comfort only at the expense of truth. They are pleasing dreams and nothing more.

Great comfort again is found by orthodoxy in the theory of special providences. When a man is overtaken by some great calamity or realises some great happiness, he is taught to attribute it to a deliberate and isolated feat of the Omnipotent will. If he comes into a fortune, it is God working for his special benefit. If he loses those dearest to him, it is a special interposition of Providence either for their advantage or the discipline of his own imperfect faith. And that a large amount of comfort is derived from such a representation by those to whom it has not yet lost its validity, can hardly be denied. It is pleasant to think that you are the special object of a divine interference in the order of things.

Another particular in which the popular religion claims superiority over rational religion, as far as comfort is concerned, is that it has an infallible authority for its beliefs, vested in Pope or Church or Bible, so that the believer is under no fear of making mistakes or missing the truth. It has all been miraculously revealed for him, and he need have no anxiety about it, as the rationalist must have, who seeks it, as the phrase goes, by "unassisted human reason." And here again we cannot deny that the comfort is real and large, if the popular religion has such an infallible authority as it claims.

Well, these are one or two points in regard to which orthodoxy claims to be superior to a religion such as ours. We can offer no magic salvation through the merits of Christ; we say but little of heaven, because we know but little; we believe in no special Providence that is not also universal; we have no comfortable assurance of a supernatural infallible authority. Before, however, we can allow the claim, we must ask the important question, "Are these comfortable doctrines of orthodoxy true?" Because, if they are not true, it is of very little consequence whether or not they are comforting. I need not stop to argue the question. We, here, have arrived at the opinion that they are not true. But I want to emphasize the fact that this question of truth must always take precedence of the question of comfort. The first question which we have to ask concerning any doctrine is not, "Is it comforting?" but "Is it true?"—and the amount of comfort which a doctrine affords is no test of its truth at all. And yet I doubt if this is the ordinary way of looking at the matter. I cannot help thinking that the first question a great many people ask about a doctrine is "Is it comfortable? Should I like to believe it?" And, then, because it is comfortable, they think it must be true. They reason in a vicious circle. They take comfort in a doctrine because they believe it to be true, and they believe it to be true because it is able to comfort them. Surely this is a great mistake. Your acceptance or rejection of a doctrine must be decided simply and solely with a view to truth. Comfort has nothing to do with it; and if you let it sway your judgment, you may be living in a mere comfortable dream. If, therefore, a man chooses orthodoxy rather than heterodoxy because he imagines its doctrines are more comforting, he is building his faith upon the sand. The popular supernaturalism may be false for all its comforting assurances. The unpopular rational religion may be true, for all its lack of superficial consolations. We must choose, not the theology we like best, but that which we think the truest.

Clearly premising, therefore, that if our Unitarianism were as deficient in comforting power as it is sometimes said to be, this fact would afford no reason whatever for rejecting it; I go on to ask the further question, "Is it wanting in comforting power? Is it the cold, vague, unsatisfying faith which we are told it is? Or, whatever orthodox comforts it may miss, has it not others of its own, and those very real and very deep?" Now, I am convinced, though this is no argument whatever for its truth, that our faith is in no way inferior to orthodoxy in respect to its power to comfort men's souls. Its comforting assurances are not the same, but there are no better to be had. They are wonderfully sweet and good. Let us see what the consolations of rational religion are.

We have no comfortable scheme of salvation, but then we have no angry God, or malignant devil, from whom we need to be saved. Sin is dreadful, not because it is followed by punishment (it would be far worse if it were not), but because it demoralizes the soul; and salvation is not escape from punishment, but the purifying of the soul through the fires of remorse. We need to be saved, not from God, but from sin; and therefore we do not require the assurance that Christ died as a propitiation to God.

We are less garrulous, less dogmatic, than our neighbours in speaking of the future life. But, therein, we really lose no true consolation, because, since no man has seen behind the veil, all descriptions are merely guesses; and we, when we say that whatever the future life may be, it will be surrounded by and filled with the love of God, are saying all that there is to be said, and it seems to me are saying enough to satisfy the heart's deepest need. It should be enough for any man to know that to die is to fall into the hands of God. We do not care much for the theory of special interpositions of Providence. And I do not think we lose much thereby, for we have the compensating belief in the general beneficence of God's universal laws. I cannot see that it greatly helps me to bear my loss to believe that I am singled out by the deliberate choice of Heaven. I would much rather feel that my loss is humanity's gain, that I am experiencing the effects of a law, which, whether I can see it or not, is beneficent in its general scope. Where I could not bow to an arbitrary will, I can to the inexorable laws which work the good of all. Only when I am sure that God does not slay me wilfully, can I say though He slay me, yet will I trust in Him. Then I can sing,

> Thy various messengers employ,
> Thy purposes of love fulfil;
> And 'mid the wreck of human joy
> Let kneeling faith adore Thy will.

And then, again, we have not the comfortable assurance of an infallible church or book to guarantee the correctness of our faith. But the comfort of this thought is of such a quality that only those who dare not, or will not take the trouble to think for themselves, really care for it. And we have as a compensating consolation, the thought that God does not require accuracy of belief as a condition of salvation, but would rather have a man be true to his own convictions, even though they be mistaken, than give a mere unthinking assent to a church's creed, however true.

You see, therefore, that even on those points where orthodoxy seems to offer special consolations, we stand at no disadvantage. But, besides this, we have other thoughts of comfort which orthodoxy knows not of, or knows but very slightly. Surely it is a source of infinite comfort to have broken down that unholy barrier between things sacred and things secular, which has made religion to so many a wearisome burden. According to the orthodox conception, religion is like a nun afraid to mingle in the world; the natural pleasures and interests of this life are all regarded with a suspicious eye as antagonistic to a devout piety, and the Delectable Mountains are always represented, as in Bunyan's story, to be situated in the other world. What a consolation to know that this is all a mistake, that there is no unholy divorce between religion and the world, that the world of sense, the world of science, the world of men, and all the natural interests and pleasures of our earthly life are pure and sacred to pure and holy souls! What a joy to feel that there is no antagonism between religion and the things of our common life! How comforting, again, to have awaked from the terrible old dream of a fallen and degraded humanity, to the new truth of a humanity developing, struggling slowly upwards, from a lower to a higher life; to believe that life is ever getting to be better worth the having, that ignorance and cruelty and injustice and oppression are being driven more and more into the corners of the earth, that mankind, in spite of many aberrations, has been advancing from the remotest past and will continue to advance to the remotest future, that every good thought or word or deed, in however obscure a corner of the world, helps to bring in the kingdom of righteousness, that past, present and future are all working together for us and for all mankind! And then what a wonderful comfort to have got rid of all religious fear and to know that God is perfect Love, to feel that there is no divine wrath to escape from, that there is only a fulness of love to apprehend! There is no despair of this life, there is no dread of death, there is no anxious doubt about eternity when once I realize that God is Love. For then I know that Love holds and embraces me, wraps me round above and below, cares for me in all times of my distress, has mapped out my eternal future as shall be the very best for me, has sent me trial and sorrow only for my exceeding blessing. True, there are mysteries in life for which I may not hold the key. I see the brave ship battered to pieces in the stormy waves, the goodly town shattered by the earthquake or buried beneath the ashes of the volcano's fire; I see hunger and nakedness, cold and pestilence, evils grim and gaunt stalking across the world, and there is weeping and gnashing of teeth. But once let me be certain that Love is the guiding force, leading the world and man by a steady progress from good to better and from better to best, and I then can look these things in the face and yet be not dismayed. There is an infinite power to comfort in the thought of God's Almighty Love. God has known of all these things, has foreseen them, has provided for them, and God is Love. All, therefore, must be well.

> These surface troubles come and go
> Like rufflings of the sea ;
> The deeper depth is out of reach
> To all, my God, but Thee.

Talk of the consolations of orthodoxy ! They are poor compared with those offered by the religion whose first article is " God is Love." Who would want an atonement, if God is love? Who would not be content to know of heaven that it is provided by a God of love ? Who would ask for special providences, if he felt that every law of the universe is a law of love ? Who would seek an infallible church or Bible to teach him that God is love ? Ah, this is comfort that cannot be shaken. Knowing this, we feel little desire to dogmatise about God, or the life to come, or schemes of salvation. God's ways are higher than our ways, and His thoughts than our thoughts. All we care to know is that they are ways and thoughts of love. That assurance brings us a calm habitual delight, a tranquillity of trust, a peculiar silent joy, for which " comfort " is altogether too small and poor a word. It is, in apostolic phrase, the peace of God which passeth understanding.

XII.

"With all your Heart."

Ye shall seek me, and find me, when ye shall search for me with all your heart.—JEREMIAH xxix., 13.

NOTHING is more striking in the history of humanity than to notice how in all times and nations men have tried to find out God. Each in his own way, peering through his own darkness, grasping some little fragment of truth, and gathering in the same effort a whole handful of dust and chaff, looking up from the shadows which encircle his own life to the light where God the Eternal Spirit dwells. There have been seekers after God in every land and age, who have striven in some fashion to solve the greatest of all questions, and to sound the deepest of all mysteries. The idol-worshipper, bowing before his image of wood or stone; the fire-worshipper, bending in lowly adoration to the sun as the sole Lord and Giver of life; the savage who dimly feels the presence of the Great Spirit in the world around him and in the restless ocean and the star-lit vault of sky, or hears a more than earthly voice in the storm and the earthquake and the thunder; the Hindoo bending low in Brahman Temple; the Mohammedan praying in Turkish Mosque; the Catholic at some sacred shrine; the monk in mediæval Minster—you may see in them all the eager yearning spirit feeling after God if haply it may find Him. And still to-day the search goes on, now perhaps more keenly, more restlessly than ever. Our days are fallen on times of doubting, questioning, examining, trying the spirits whether they be of God. Men take less on trust than once they did. They are intent on probing the whole mystery, and getting to know the exact truth about

God. And so they search and argue and debate, climb the heights of thought and sound the depths of knowledge, and pry into every corner if may be they may find some certain evidence of a present God. And yet sometimes, the more they examine and investigate, the further they seem to be from the object of their search; the more they seek God, the further they seem to wander from him; the more they inquire, the more they doubt. And this is the case not only in the mere externals and accidents of religion—things which perhaps it may be well to lose one's faith in; the difficulty goes deeper. The clouds and the darkness begin to veil the heavens, and men are not sure whether there be any God behind them, or whether the clouds and the darkness are all.

Now how is this? Is the search for God, the desire not to take any theory of religion on trust, but to get to know the divine secret for oneself, a dangerous and hopeless quest? Does faith die the moment you begin to uncover its roots? Is it better to shut one's eyes and mutter some worn-out creed? Or is there some good reason why the modern spirit of investigation so often leads a man into unbelief?

I cannot help thinking that there is some hint of an explanation in the words which I have taken for my text, "Ye shall seek me and find me, when ye shall search for me with all your heart." Our modern investigations are too coldly intellectual. Men are seeking God by the intellect, the reasoning faculties, when He is only to be found by the heart. They are trying to break open the sacred ark with the chisel of logic, when it will only yield to the golden key of love. Their search may well be fruitless. God does not reveal Himself to those who seek Him so.

We live, you must remember, in days when the world is nothing if not scientific. But not all knowledge is reached that way. I have a most profound respect for science. The truths she has revealed, the errors she has destroyed, the services she has rendered to humanity are almost countless; and I believe that her teachings prepare and point the way to a higher and sublimer conception of God than any you can find in the creeds. But though science may point the way, though you may draw the noblest religious inferences from modern scientific discoveries; by science you can never reach religious knowledge. It is not the business of science to teach religion. It is the business of science to seek the causes of things in the universe of things, and a resort to the supernatural would, from her point of view, be a confession of ignorance. Science and religion are both seekings after truth, but in very different ways. Science seeks with the senses and the understanding, with computation and deduction and analysis. Religion seeks with the trusting heart and devout aspiration. The aim of the one is conquest; the aim of the other is surrender. Science seeks to extend the realm of physical knowledge; religion is content to bow low in the presence of an Infinite Unknown. And so God cannot be laid hold of by the methods of scientific inquiry, and it is only when the eye of speculation is shut that the heart finds Him who is personally related to every soul.

May not this have something to do with the fruitlessness of much modern seeking after God? There are hundreds of men to-day who have sought for God and have not found Him, just because they have never fulfilled the one essential condition that they should seek for Him with "all their heart." They have argued about religion, discussed religious questions, attended theological lectures, read theological treatises; but their belief, if belief they have, is simply a cold, heartless, speculative, unprofitable thing—a mere assent to an intellectual proposition, not a warm, living, life-giving affection of the heart. They do not turn to God in all their troubles and sorrows and perplexities, and seek the refuge of His love. They do not go to Him for comfort and guidance and counsel. They do not trust Him in all the dark seasons of their life. He hardly comes into their real life at all. He is only an abstract theory. He is not a heart-felt fact. Such do not and cannot find God in any real sense at all. The men and women who really find God may be very poor theologians, but they have felt the power of His Spirit working in their souls. They are those who cry with the Psalmist, " As the hart panteth after the water-brooks, so panteth my soul after Thee, O God." The thought of God comes into all their life, mingles with all that is deepest and tenderest in their nature, touches their every hope and joy, their every sorrow, pain and fear. They draw near to God in every grief. They take counsel with Him in every difficulty. They give thanks to Him when their heart is glad. They seek rest in Him when their souls are weary; and the thought that He is ever close at hand to help them, that His presence surrounds them always, and that in Him they live and move and have their being is a thought of continual joy and peace. They look at the wonders of nature, and they say, " My Father created them." They gaze into the starry sky, and they say, " He is there too. His presence reaches into the furthest region of imaginable space, and yet is so present here that not a sparrow falleth to the ground without His will. He dwells on high in unseen glory, and yet is close to me—His earthly child. And whatever marvel of His doings in distant star and sun science may lead me to infer and guess, yet this I surely know, that he never ceases to hold my hand in His, or to whisper to my soul the eternal message of His love." Such souls have found God and can never lose Him, because whenever the intellectual path to Him is blocked by some apparent obstacle, the spiritual way is still open, and it is with them, as it was with him who sang,

> If e'er when faith had fallen asleep
> I heard a voice ' Believe no more,'
> And heard an everbreaking shore
> That tumbled in the Godless deep;
>
> A warmth within the breast would melt
> The freezing reason's colder part,
> And like a man in wrath, the heart
> Stood up and answered, ' I have felt.'

And, you will notice, that this spiritual knowledge of God, this seeking and finding Him with the heart, is open to all alike. The wise and the learned and the intellectual giants are no better furnished for the search than the simple, the humble and the poor. God does not say I will reveal Myself when you seek for Me with all the strength of a mighty intellect, but simply " when you search for me with all your heart." The strength of reasoning, the force of genius, the resources of human learning—these are not the proper implements of religion, and it is not by such searching that you will find out the Almighty. Often He hides Himself from the well-equipped philosopher and the learned theologian, and reveals Himself to those who are babes in intellectual wisdom, but have sought Him with all the burning love and aspiration of their souls.

This, it seems to me, is a fact of which the world to-day needs reminding. Many a plain, unlettered man or woman, many an untutored youth, many a simple girl, is standing aghast at the ever rising hill of knowledge, and the ever deepening flood of questions and arguments, theories and disputations, that bar the theological road, and is asking despairingly, "How, amid all this maze of theology and these interminable discussions, is a plain man or woman to find the way to God?" And, I dare say that there are some who hear me now, who, looking at all the writing and speaking bearing on the philosophy of religion that is going on to-day, reading now this essay now that article, and finding themselves only the more perplexed, with neither time nor knowledge sufficient to attempt to bottom the matter for themselves, and perceiving that those who have both, arrive at differing conclusions, are utterly appalled and discouraged by the difficulties of theological research, and are tempted to think that it is of no use seeking to gain any clear religious light. Friends, believe me, it is not necessary to be great theologians in order to reach a sure knowledge of God. I do not want to disparage theology. All these great and difficult questions that are being discussed to-day are important enough, and have their due influence on our religious ideas. But you can find God very certainly without waiting to settle all these. All that is needed is that you bring to the quest not merely an intellectual curiosity, but the strength and fervour of your heart's life and love. You may not be able to see your way through all the problems that perplexed the men of science and theology, you may not be able to give a very logical account of your religious faith ; but if you have opened your whole heart to God, and held communion with Him in your inmost soul, and have made His constant help a real part of your life, then you will have reached a knowledge of God deeper than any process

of reasoning could give you—you will have found God
Himself, and that is worth more than any theory about Him.
It is with religion as it is with music. There is the theory
of music, and the music itself. The one you can make a
matter of intellectual study, but the other you simply listen
to, and it enters into your soul. The man who is ignorant
of the theory may yet accept and enjoy the music. But the
man whose life is spent in perpetual silence will know
nothing of music, though he may have the whole theory of
it at his finger-ends. So with religion. There is the theory
of religion, theology; and there is religion itself, a living
communion with God. The one is a matter of the intellect;
the other is a thing of the heart. And the soul that
communes with God, finds Him, however poor be its
theology; whereas the man who lives in spiritual silence,
though he be the skilfullest theologian, really knows nothing
of God Himself. Be not over-troubled, therefore, by the
multitude of theological questions that are springing up
every day and waiting for solution. Do your best to solve
them, as far as it is in your power; but though you fail, still
remember that the saying is true to day and for ever, " Ye
shall seek me, and find me, when ye shall search for me with
all your heart."

The first thing, therefore, that I wish to urge to-day
is that we must seek God in the right way; not as an
intellectual hypothesis, but as a spiritual fact, to be realised
by the loving heart, not demonstrated by a cold and
rigid logic.

But the words I have chosen suggest another condition, if
we are to be successful in our search. We must seek " with
all our heart." No half-hearted seeking will serve. " Ye
shall find me, when ye shall search for me with *all* your heart."
Friends, is it much to be wondered at that a good many of
us fail in finding God? Why, if you could read the lives of
all the people gathered in the churches and chapels of this
city to-day, in how many of them would you find a whole-
hearted seeking after God? I know, you know, we all know
that the religion of hundreds and thousands of them is the
poorest, most miserable, most contemptibly half-hearted thing
imaginable. This is the secret of our religious poverty. We

take censuses, we lament our half-filled churches, we discuss our church organisations, the modes of our services, the methods of our church work; we hold meetings and read papers, and plan first this scheme and then that, and the question that is always before us is, "What's the matter?" What is wrong with our religious life? Friends, this is the matter with it, this is wrong with it, and this sums up nearly all the mischief—it is half-hearted; we are only half in earnest in our seeking after God. And when we have said that, we have said enough to explain the greater part of our difficulties, for the prophet's words are equally true in their negative form, " Ye shall seek me, and ye shall not find me, until ye shall search for me with all your heart." We don't deserve to find God, seeking for Him in such miserable fashion as many of us do. This is an old cry, I know. All this has been said many times before. But it is the thing that wants saying, the great lesson that the world to-day needs to learn —that this unearnest playing with religion is utterly useless, that faith in God is a thing not worth speaking of unless a man put into it his whole heart and mind and strength. I am not a great stickler for the outward expressions of the religious life, but straws will show how the wind is blowing. Why should people allow circumstances to keep them away from church, which they would never think of allowing to interfere with a concert or an evening party? Why, when a man is a little over busy, should his religious work, his charitable labours, or his Sunday School class, be the first engagement he gives up? Why, when a child is to be educated, is religious teaching the last thing thought of or provided for? And why, if French or music lessons clash with a Bible class, is it always the latter that is foregone? Why, if a ball and a religious meeting happen on the same night, is it at once assumed that the religious meeting and not the ball will suffer? Such things are trifles in themselves, but they are indications of a more serious fact, the fact that with a vast number of professedly religious people, religion holds only a secondary place. It is something which they put in when everything has been attended to; the first thing to be left out when something must go. In other words their religion is half-hearted. It is the element of their life which they believe in, not rather more, but rather less, than all the rest. No wonder their vision of divine realities is dim.

Oh, friends, let it not be so with any of us; let us surrender our whole hearts to God. Only thus can we surely find Him. He accepts no half-allegiance, He is satisfied with no divided service. He must be sought first and last, at the beginning and at the end. Come, therefore, you whose lives are still fresh and young, with the morning dew still glistening on your feet and your powers of love and reverence still untarnished in your hearts, come while it is still easy to seek God and find Him ; before the trumpet summons you to life's great battle, and the sky is clouded with smoke and dust, and the darkness and confusion hide your way, —come and consecrate your strength to God.

And come you, too, for whom the shadows are lengthening, as even now you stand amid life's din and tumult—if perchance you have never found God in any deep, real way (have heard about Him and read about Him and talked about Him, but have never found Him for yourself)—come you also; it is not too late to find Him, if you will only seek Him with all your heart.

Yes, one and all, seek ye God with heart and soul and strength. For then you shall win a peace which God alone can give and nothing can take away. It shall lie so deep that the storms and troubles of life shall pass over it and move it not; and beneath all the surface waves that toss the feeble-hearted, your steadfast souls shall ever lie calm and still.

> The surface troubles come and go
> Like rufflings of the sea ;
> The deeper depth is out of reach
> To all, my God, but Thee.

XIII.

Faith Overcoming the World.

For whatsoever is born of God overcometh the world: and this is the victory that overcometh the world, even our faith.—I. JOHN v., 4.

LIVING, as we do, in a land and an age which call themselves Christian; a land filled with Christian institutions, an age when it is no hardship but only the ordinary fashionable thing to do to confess the name of Christ; it is by no means easy to realise what being a Christian meant in apostolic days, when Judaism was the fashion, and Christianity a despised little sect. Try, however, to imagine how the new movement would strike an orthodox Pharisee or Sadducee; think of the sarcastic contempt or pitying curiosity with which he would regard this little revival among the poorer classes, how he would smile at the audacity of these enthusiastic fishermen, how he would despise their visionary fanaticism, how he would predict a speedy failure for their new-fangled designs. "It will not last," he would say: "it is the flash of a momentary enthusiasm, the passing excitement of a popular craze. As for its leader, this wild dreamer of Nazareth, this foolish carpenter's son, so pitifully ignorant of the world; his violent denunciations are transgressing the bounds of public order; we shall have to get rid of him;

and then the leader being gone, the movement will soon die out." And no doubt, after the crucifixion, he would conclude that the heresy had been crushed, and that Jerusalem had heard the last of it.

But in a few months he would hear to his surprise that the flame had burst forth again, that these fishermen and their followers had re-appeared, and were proclaiming that this man, Jesus, was the Messiah and calling upon all men to own him as the Christ ; that moreover numbers were joining the band every day, and that altogether the movement, so far from being crushed, was assuming larger proportions than ever. And then he would either join his fellow-religionists in persecuting these revivalists from city to city ; or else, believing like Gamaliel, that persecution would be the very thing to add strength to the movement, he would treat it with supreme indifference, confident that like other revivals he had witnessed, it would soon break down and disappear.

On the one hand bitter persecution, on the other indifferent contempt—that was what being a Christian meant in the apostolic age ; and yet, in spite of it all, in spite of opposition, in spite of ridicule, in spite of their poverty, their want of influence, their small numbers, these Christians, this handful of poor despised men and women in a Jewish city, conceived the grandest idea, and set before them the most gigantic aim that the world has ever wondered at. It was no less than this : to prove, right in the teeth of the feeling of the times, right in the teeth of the spirit of the whole world, that Jew, Greek, and Roman were all alike wrong ; that all existing religions must pass away ; that this new religion of theirs, this Christianity, this faith of Jesus of Nazareth, was a religion suitable for all nations, and destined to conquer the world. They solemnly and deliberately proposed to revolutionize the whole world, to alter the thoughts, feelings, and habits established by centuries ; to make a brand new society upon the earth. How the worldly-wise of that day must have smiled at their seeming folly ! And yet they entered on their undertaking in no despairing mood, but with a confident assurance of victory. It was no blind hasty demonstration. They had sat down and carefully counted the cost, and they knew what they were about.

They were not going to be discouraged by any outward results. Jesus had told them they would be most victorious when most seemingly defeated. And so they set themselves resolutely and unflinchingly to live, to suffer, if need be to die, for their cause. They determined, a little band of weak men and women, to overcome the world. Though they perished they knew that they would conquer; they knew that whatsoever is born of God can overcome the world. And so, absurd though their attempt must have seemed to the ordinary Jew or Gentile, they did conquer; they did overcome the world; and before the assault of this handful of Christians, the systems of Judaism and Paganism crumbled into dust.

And if you seek to find out the cause of their success; if you want to know the weapons with which they fought; or the means which they employed to gain their victory; you will find that it was all explained by one of them when he said, "This is the victory that overcometh the world, even our faith." It was the faith which was in the hearts of those early Christians, a faith borne witness to by many a brave confession, by many a glad and glorious martyrdom; just this and nothing else, that won the world to Christ. You can almost understand it, when you listen to the great ringing words in which that faith found utterance, "Yea, we are a wonder to you," cries the fiery Tertullian in his splendid audacity. "We conquer when we are killed. You may call us food of the faggots, and may burn us, bound to the stake in the circle of fire. That is the fashion of our victory; that is our festal array; that is the chariot in which we ride out our triumph." So again the cry of this victory leapt from the lips of St. Ignatius. "Close to the swords, and close to God! In the midst of the wild beasts, and in the midst of God!"

I believe it may be taken as an established fact that on the whole and in the end the victory always falls to those who have the largest amount of faith. Faith removes whole mountains of opposition. In every undertaking, from the smallest effort of the smallest life to the preaching of a gospel, they conquer who believe in their mission and their work. Of course for the victory to be permanent the cause must be a righteous one. But even faith in a bad cause wins a quick though not a lasting triumph. Faith in a good cause wins a victory slowly as a rule, but a victory that endures. It never falters, it never relaxes in its efforts, it is never discouraged by temporary defeat or seeming failure; it is satisfied as to the goodness of its cause and it knows that whatsoever is born of God overcometh the world.

Seeing then what a mighty thing this faith is as a motive power, and comparing Christianity as it is to-day with Christianity in its early days; we need hardly be altogether in the dark as to what is the matter with our nineteenth century religion. For surely something is the matter with it, or rather with us; else we should not see the churches fighting so feebly as they do against the wickedness and spiritual darkness of the world; gaining an inch here, giving an inch there, and losing souls almost as fast as they win them; we should not see them doing what is infinitely worse, making a truce with evil and agreeing to live on good terms with mammon; we should not be content, as most of us are, to see the churches going one way and the world going quite another.

This is the matter with us. Christianity is now as often a fashion as a conviction, and we have not, as a rule, the old faith, which is the sole secret of victory. Our worst ills come from our want of confidence in our religion. We only half believe in it. We begin to think that it is—well a little unpractical, very good in its way, but not quite the thing to rule all our life, not quite the thing to conquer all the world. We hardly know it, but we are a little bit ashamed of it, and we like to keep it as much as possible inside our churches and not to talk too loudly about it in the world. It is owing to this half-hearted faith that the word runs somewhat slowly in these days of ours. Where do you think Christianity would have been if its first disciples had been what we call average Christians. I doubt if it would ever have got out of Palestine. Our feeble triumphs are easily accounted for when we note the difference between our modern easy-going Christians and the men and women who left all to follow in the steps of Christ. It is not that Christianity is less fitted for the world now than it was then; it is not that the world is less ready to receive it; it is that those who bear witness to it are lacking in faith. Writes William Bell Scott

> "Follow me," Jesus said; and they uprose,
> Peter and Andrew rose and followed him,
> Followed him even to heaven through death most grim,
> And through a long, hard life without repose
> Save in the grand ideal of its close.
> "Take up your cross and come with me," he said,
> And the world listens yet through all her dead,
> And still would answer, had we faith like those!

It is to me a most marvellous thing to notice how many people to-day profess discipleship to Jesus Christ, profess allegiance to Christian principles, and yet never seem in the least moved by that Christian faith whose first object always is to conquer and redeem the world. Whatever form of Christianity a man holds, whether he be orthodox or heterodox, there is that in his Christianity which can save men from sin, and if he believes in his religion at all he must know that. Christianity is not a philosophy. It is a spirit and a life. And it is good for all times and all people. Here are plain Christian principles bearing directly on the needs of modern society, and here is a society full of misery and weariness and sin because it has not yet learnt those principles, and it seems to me that the very stones should cry out against the man who, knowing the might of these principles, does not set to work to apply them and spread them in the world. I care not whether he be Trinitarian or Unitarian, Churchman or Methodist, if he be honest he must believe that his Christianity is just the simplest and most truthful form of religion, and therefore most fitted to overcome the world. And how, believing that, he can remain quietly indifferent whether this faith of his does overcome or not is a problem which only modern Christians can solve. A world to redeem and glorify. Thousands of men and women every Sunday professing a religion which is able to redeem and glorify it. And yet hardly one in ten of them seriously setting about to carry out the redemption. That is the curious spectacle presented by nineteenth century Christianity. How is it to be accounted for? You have heard of "arm-chair politicians." Well, I take it, it is because so many of us are " arm-chair " Christians, just content to sit in our cushioned pews and willing to do little else. And I fear that our liberal churches are especially open to this charge. I fear that very often we sit still and congratulate ourselves complacently on our enlightened views, which we say the world is not ready for, when we ought to be preaching our Christianity, whatever it is, in the sure faith that whatsoever is born of God overcometh the world.

Brethren, we want deep conviction; we want the spirit of Christianity in larger measure to quicken us into a more vigorous religious life. We boast of our freedom, but all our freedom is of no use to us, unless we get that. You may have spiritual deadness, religious apathy, narrow sympathies, and a cold faith in connection with a free and enlightened theology, as well as in the bondage of cramping creeds. You may unbind a corpse, but it will not move, and you may give a man theological liberty, but that alone will not quicken his spiritual life. We must have faith as well as freedom.

But, you may depend upon it, we shall neither get it nor keep it, by trying to nurse it among ourselves. There is no vainer thought than to imagine that you can sit down and live upon what faith you have got. Unless you are willing to share it you will never keep it. Unless you are willing to go forth, strong in its might, to overcome the evil of the world, you will soon find that it will droop and die.

One other thought take with you. This true living faith overcomes not only the world around us, but the world within us, the worldly spirit in our hearts. When you really believe in the religion of Jesus Christ, the religion of perfect love, you cannot live a selfish worldly life. The love of personal ease, of pleasure, of position, of wealth, are all subdued by a greater love; and, by your faith, you rise above them and win the victory over every worldly thought. And a victory there must be one way or the other. Either we must overcome the world, or the world will overcome us. If we put our whole hearts into our business or our pleasure, our money-making or our own enjoyment, if our whole love flows out " to things so soiled and dim," we lose the battle, and, if never before, we shall learn in the hour of death that the world has wrested all our wealth from us ;—and we shall enter heaven as paupers.

If, on the other hand, while using and enjoying the world and its riches and pleasures, we steadfastly keep our hearts above them; always working with a holy purpose, always giving our richest love to God ; then we overcome the world. We win a peace which the world cannot take away. We have treasures in heaven, to which death gives us the inheritance. Leaving the world we leave what we no longer want. We pass to a larger life. We go to a fuller love. We triumph over the world, because faith has given us the victory.

PRINTED AT THE MERCURY PRESS, BEDFORD.

www.ingramcontent.com/pod-product-compliance
Lightning Source LLC
Chambersburg PA
CBHW020158170426
43199CB00010B/1090